Grade 8

Addison-Wesley Mathematics

Building Thinking Skills Workbook

▲▼ Addison-Wesley Publishing Company

Menlo Park, California ■ Reading, Massachusetts ■ New York
Don Mills, Ontario ■ Wokingham, England ■ Amsterdam ■ Bonn
Sydney ■ Singapore ■ Tokyo ■ Madrid ■ San Juan

ISBN 0-201-27819-7

ABCDEFGHIJKL-HC-96543210

Table of Contents

Name _____

Understanding Bar Graphs

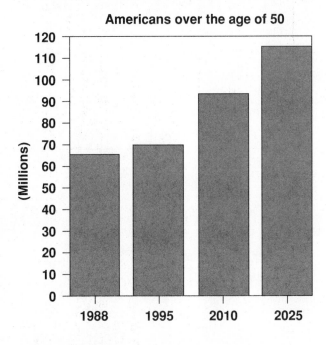

Americans over the age of 50

(chart y-axis label: (Millions); y-axis values: 0, 10, 20, 30, 40, 50, 60, 70, 80, 90, 100, 110, 120; x-axis values: 1988, 1995, 2010, 2025)

In the future, the number of Americans over the age of 50 is expected to increase.

Use the graph to answer these questions.
Round answers to the nearest 5 million.

1. How many Americans were over the age of 50 in 1988?

_____

2. How many Americans will be over the age of 50 in 2010?

_____

3. How many more Americans over the age of 50 will there be in 2025 than in 1988?

_____

4. Between which years was there the greatest increase in the number of Americans over the age of 50?

_____

5. In what year on the graph will you be over the age of 50? How many Americans will be over the age of 50 along with you?

_____

Name _____

Number Properties

Do you think the following properties hold for all
real numbers? Give an example.

1. $7 - 4 \overset{?}{=} 4 - 7$

Is subtraction commutative? _____

Example:

_____

2. $(18 \div 6) \div 2 \overset{?}{=} 18 \div (6 \div 2)$

Is division associative? _____

Example:

_____

3. $20 \div 5 \overset{?}{=} 5 \div 20$

Is division commutative? _____

Example:

_____

4. $6 + (8 \times 3) \overset{?}{=} (6 + 8) \times (6 + 3)$

Is addition distributive
over multiplication? _____

Example:

_____

5. $9 \times (5 - 2) \overset{?}{=} (9 \times 5) - (9 \times 2)$

Is multiplication
distributive over subtraction? _____

Example:

_____

6. $22 \div 1 \overset{?}{=} 22$

Is 1 the identity for division? _____

Example:

_____

7. Marty the messed-up mathematician uses
these two examples to prove that addition
and multiplication are always the same:

$0 + 0 = 0$ and $0 \times 0 = 0$
$2 + 2 = 4$ and $2 \times 2 = 4$

If a rule works for a certain pair of
numbers, will it work for any pair of
numbers?

_____

Make up your own example to show that
Marty's conclusion is false.

_____

Name _____

Subtraction Shortcut

Roberto discovered a new way to subtract.

$$
\begin{array}{r}
623 \\
-\ 96 \\
\end{array}
\qquad
\begin{array}{r}
623 \\
-\ 100 \\
\hline
523 \\
+\quad 4 \\
\hline
527 \\
\end{array}
$$

96 = 100 − 4

$$
\begin{array}{r}
462 \\
-\ 298 \\
\end{array}
\qquad
\begin{array}{r}
462 \\
-\ 300 \\
\hline
162 \\
+\quad 2 \\
\hline
164 \\
\end{array}
$$

298 = 300 − 2

Use Roberto's method to find the differences.

1.
$$
\begin{array}{r}
212 \\
-\ 93 \\
\end{array}
$$

2.
$$
\begin{array}{r}
716 \\
-\ 389 \\
\end{array}
$$

3.
$$
\begin{array}{r}
451 \\
-\ 97 \\
\end{array}
$$

4.
$$
\begin{array}{r}
634 \\
-\ 198 \\
\end{array}
$$

5.
$$
\begin{array}{r}
832 \\
-\ 288 \\
\end{array}
$$

6.
$$
\begin{array}{r}
3{,}261 \\
-\ 1{,}998 \\
\end{array}
$$

Solve mentally using Roberto's method. Write only your answers.

7. $762 - 99 =$ _____

8. $284 - 95 =$ _____

9. $316 - 97 =$ _____

10. $623 - 88 =$ _____

11. $557 - 89 =$ _____

12. $821 - 85 =$ _____

13. $418 - 198 =$ _____

14. $523 - 293 =$ _____

15. $312 - 196 =$ _____

16. $2{,}354 - 295 =$ _____

17. $1{,}867 - 398 =$ _____

18. $3{,}914 - 3{,}687 =$ _____

Name _____

Wrong Number

Five of the following sums or differences are wrong.
Find them by estimating. Circle the incorrect equations.

1. $38 + 53 = 91$

2. $83 + 75 = 158$

3. $308 + 479 = 987$

4. $19{,}274 + 14{,}009 = 33{,}283$

5. $63{,}418 - 44{,}312 = 11{,}106$

6. $41 + 56 + 78 = 175$

7. $773 - 147 = 326$

8. $125 - 62 = 63$

9. $99 + 102 + 105 + 98 = 404$

10. $456 + 139 = 794$

11. $4{,}618 - 734 = 3{,}884$

12. $23 + 25 + 21 + 29 = 218$

Five of the following products or quotients are wrong.
Find them by estimating. Circle the incorrect equations.

13. $5{,}629 \times 32 = 180{,}128$

14. $53 \times 27 = 2{,}431$

15. $720 \div 8 = 90$

16. $1{,}113 \div 21 = 53$

17. $6{,}256 \div 92 = 88$

18. $9 \times 312 = 2{,}808$

19. $79 \times 48 = 3{,}792$

20. $280 \div 40 = 70$

21. $12 \times 61 = 832$

22. $3{,}792 \times 408 = 1{,}547{,}136$

23. $5{,}751 \div 81 = 71$

24. $17{,}652 \div 39 = 652$

Name _____

Operating Differently

New operations are frequently developed by mathematicians.
The new operations below require 2 steps. Analyze each definition
and use it to find answers.

1. * means to find the sum of the numbers and then multiply
the sum by 3.

Example: $2 * 3 = (2 + 3) \times 3 = 15$

$7 * 2 =$ _____ $11 * 5 =$ _____ $8 * 6 =$ _____
$2 * 7 =$ _____ $3 * 3 =$ _____ $25 * 30 =$ _____

2. # means to find the product of the numbers and then add 6.

Example: $6 \# 7 = (6 \times 7) + 6 = 48$

$3 \# 8 =$ _____ $7 \# 8 =$ _____ $23 \# 1 =$ _____
$20 \# 5 =$ _____ $45 \# 2 =$ _____ $55 \# 5 =$ _____

3. @ means to find the sum of the numbers. If the sum is
even, write 0. If the sum is odd, write 1.

Example: $3 @ 2 = 3 + 2$ is odd $= 1$

$4 @ 6 =$ _____ $6 @ 7 =$ _____ $8 @ 3 =$ _____
$45 @ 34 =$ _____ $71 @ 65 =$ _____ $89 @ 12 =$ _____

4. $ means to subract the numbers (in any order) and then
multiply the answer by itself.

Example: $7 \$ 18 = (18 - 7) \times (18 - 7) = 11 \times 11 = 121$

$23 \$ 16 =$ _____ $23 \$ 20 =$ _____ $15 \$ 5 =$ _____
$12 \$ 4 =$ _____ $5 \$ 10 =$ _____ $24 \$ 31 =$ _____

5. Examine the set of examples below. Then find the missing
answers. Write a definition for the new operation.

$2 !! 3 = 13$ $3 !! 3 = 18$ $4 !! 5 = 41$
$4 !! 6 = 52$ $3 !! 7 = 58$ $10 !! 5 = 125$
$6 !! 2 =$ _____ $8 !! 1 =$ _____ $5 !! 9 =$ _____

Definition _____

_____

Find the Flaws

Each of these students' work shows a pattern of mistakes.

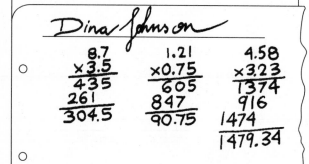

Ed Samuels

```
  1.45        2.45       43.6
×20.2        ×403       ×20.8
  290         735       3488
  000         000        000
  290         980        872
3.190      105.35     122.08
```

Dina Johnson

```
   8.7        1.21        4.58
 ×3.5       ×0.75        ×3.23
  435         605        1374
  261         847         916
304.5       90.75        1474
                       1479.34
```

Josh Edwards

```
        2            2
  4.2         6.3          74
 ×6.4        ×17        ×3.6
 2.48         8.1        234
```

Sandra Long

```
   5.6         7.8        1.23
  ×3.4        ×27        ×4.2
 2024        4956         246
 1518        1416        4812
172.04      1911.6     48.266
```

1. What is Ed doing wrong?

_____

_____

2. Go back and write the correct product below each exercise.

3. What is Dina doing wrong?

_____

_____

4. Go back and write the correct product below each exercise.

5. What is Josh doing wrong?

_____

_____

6. Go back and write the correct product below each exercise.

7. What is Sandra doing wrong?

_____

_____

8. Go back and write the correct product below each exercise.

Name _____

Math Express

Use the given numbers and operations once each to
write an expression. You may use parentheses.

Write an expression equal to 27.

$$(3 \times 5) + (6 \times 2)$$

1.

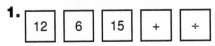

Write an expression equal to 13.

2.

Write an expression equal to 11.

3.

| 6 | 8 | 4 | × | ÷ |

Write an expression equal to 12.

4.

| 7 | 6 | 3 | × | + |

Write an expression equal to 63.

5.

| 3 | 7 | 9 | 4 | + | + | − |

Write an expression equal to 5.

6.

| 4 | 5 | 9 | 16 | + | − | ÷ |

Write an expression equal to 0.

7.

| 2 | 3 | 10 | 15 | ÷ | ÷ | − |

Write an expression equal to 0.

8.

| 1 | 3 | 27 | 81 | − | ÷ | ÷ |

Write an expression equal to 8.

9.

| 5 | 8 | 9 | 7 | + | ÷ | + |

Write an expression equal to 10.

10.

| 8 | 72 | 4 | 28 | + | ÷ | ÷ |

Write an expression equal to 16.

Alternate Keys

Read each problem and think about how you would solve
it using a calculator. However, for each problem, one key
on the calculator is broken. Explain how you would solve
each problem using the broken calculator.

1. Two track team members were comparing
pulse rates after a race. The difference
between their rates was 27 beats per
minute. The faster rate was 116 beats
per minute. What was the slower rate?
(The − key is broken.)

_____

_____

_____

_____

2. A mile relay team took 3 minutes 48
seconds (228 seconds) to complete a race.
If each team member ran for exactly 38
seconds, how many members were on the
team? (The ÷ key is broken.)

_____

_____

_____

_____

_____

3. A four-member relay team ran the quarter
mile. Each member ran exactly 11.5
seconds. How long did it take the team to
complete the race? (The × key is broken.)

_____

_____

_____

4. The grandstand at the track has 466 seats
in 8 sections. If 7 of the sections have 63
seats apiece, how many seats are in the
eighth section? (The × key is broken.)

_____

_____

_____

5. For field day the eighth grade was divided into 6 teams
of 14. There were 13 students left to form the seventh team.
How many students participated in all? (The × key is broken.)

_____

_____

_____

Create a Problem

Use the data below. Write a word problem that requires an exact answer or an estimate. Then solve your own problem.

Helpful Hints

Estimate
About how much is needed?
Is that enough?
Approximately how many?

Exact
How much more is needed?
How much change will she get back?
How many are needed?

1. Write a problem requiring an exact answer.
a pair of tennis shoes that cost $14.95
$20 bill

_____

_____

2. Write a problem where an estimate is acceptable. 6 cans of fruit at $1.49 each
$10

_____

_____

3. Write a problem requiring an exact answer.
earnings at the rate of $3.50 an hour
5 hours of work
$25.95 for a video tape

_____

_____

4. Write a problem where an estimate is acceptable. 129 tickets sold
bleachers that seat 14 people each

_____

_____

5. Write a problem requiring an exact answer.
a sweater that cost $17.95
a school binder that cost $2.95
6% sales tax
$20 bill

_____

_____

Puzzled Expressions

Evaluate each of these expressions. Substitute 12 for each variable.

1. $2w$

_____

2. $7 + x$

_____

3. $c - 3$

_____

4. $\frac{t}{2}$

_____

5. $3n - 1$

_____

Evaluate each of these expressions. Substitute 9 for each variable.

6. $2x + 3$

_____

7. $\frac{18}{m} + 4$

_____

8. $\frac{r - 1}{2}$

_____

9. $3(s + 1)$

_____

10. $23 - 2w$

_____

Evaluate each of these expressions. Substitute 20 for each variable.

11. $2p - 10$

_____

12. $4(c - 2)$

_____

13. $\frac{3 + m}{2}$

_____

14. $\frac{35 - t}{2}$

_____

15. $\frac{4n}{5}$

_____

Write three expressions equal to 15. Give the value of each variable.

16. _____

$t = $ _____

17. _____

$m = $ _____

18. _____

$w = $ _____

Write 3 expressions equal to 3. Give the value of each variable.

19. _____

$x = $ _____

20. _____

$c = $ _____

21. _____

$r = $ _____

Name _____

Electronically Speaking

The divided bar graph shows the percent of American homes having different electronics devices for two years, 1986 and 1989.

Below the graph are a number of conclusions that have been drawn from it. Some are accurate. Others need a change if they are to reflect the information in the graph. Decide which ones need changing and correct them. If you cannot tell from the graph, write **cannot tell.**

Percent of American Homes with Electronics Devices

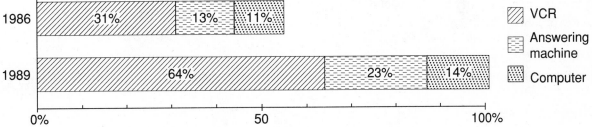

1986 | 31% | 13% | 11%
1989 | 64% | 23% | 14%

0%   50   100%

Legend: VCR, Answering machine, Computer

1. From 1986 to 1989 the percent of homes with a VCR more than doubled.

_____

2. A larger percent of homes had an answering machine in 1986 than had a computer in 1989.

_____

3. The smallest percent change from 1986 to 1989 was for computers.

_____

4. In 1986 people who owned an answering machine did not own a computer.

_____

5. In 1989 more than two thirds of all homes had a VCR.

_____

6. One hundred one percent of homes had either a VCR, an answering machine, or a computer in 1989.

_____

7. More people watched TV in 1989 than in 1986.

_____

Name _____

Career Circle

The circle graph below is correctly filled in
with the percentages. The career that belongs
in each section, however, has been left out.
Use the information below the graph to fill in
the individual sections with the correct career.
Choose from the list at the right.

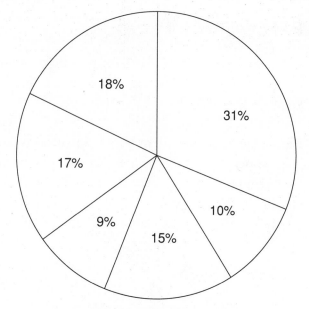

The largest section of the graph belonged to
students choosing careers other than the five
above. More students chose Business than
Engineering, Medicine, Teaching, or Law
Students chose Medicine more often than
Teaching, but less often than Engineering.
Of the five careers, only Law was chosen by
fewer students than Teaching.

**Career Choices of
High School Students**

Now answer these questions about the completed graph.
Exactly 2,000 students were included in the survey.

Engineering
Law
Medicine
Teaching
Business
Other

1. How many chose engineering? _____

2. Which careers were chosen by fewer than 300 students?

_____

3. One career choice was selected by 20 more students than another career choice.
Which pairs of careers satisfy this statement?

_____

4. How could you have answered Question 3 without
calculating the number of students who chose each career?

_____

Misleading Statistics

Lois and Harold each made an interval graph using the data below.

Years of Service for Teachers in Our School

Mr. Page	1	Ms. Reiner	6	Miss Han	8	Mrs. Kozar	8
Mrs. Green	22	Mr. O'Neil	19	Ms. Burns	5	Mr. Moore	11
Ms. Dean	9	Mr. Garcia	15	Ms. Hinks	6	Miss Parks	7
Mrs. Kanaka	2	Mrs. Judd	15	Mr. Spasky	17	Ms. Diaz	4

1. Finish each graph.

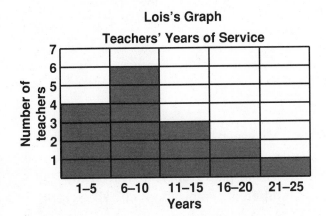

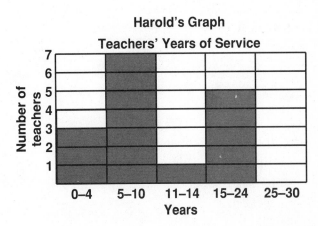

2. How is Lois's graph different from Harold's graph? Which graph gives a more useful picture

of the teachers' years of service? _____

_____

_____

3.

NL stock	Week	1	2	3	4	5
	Price	$24.00	$23.25	$23.00	$22.75	$22.00

Use the data in the chart. Draw
a graph to support one of these
statements:

A NL stock prices have fallen
dramatically over the past 5 weeks.

B NL stock prices have declined
gradually over the past 5 weeks.

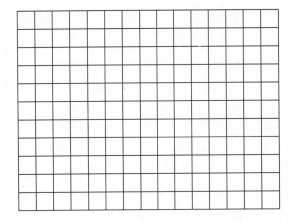

Solve It Your Way

These problems all have one thing in common: they can be solved in more than one way. Think about an appropriate strategy. Then solve each problem.

1. Twelve players are entered in a tennis tournament. If a player is eliminated after one loss, how many matches will be needed to determine a champion?

_____

2. A bag contains 9 blue chips, 7 green chips, and 11 red chips. If you choose some without looking, what is the smallest number you must choose to be certain of having at least 4 of the same color?

_____

3. It takes a plumber 12 minutes to saw a pipe into 7 sections. How long would it take her to cut the same pipe into 9 sections?

_____

4. Michael has 5 books that he is anxious to read this summer, but he has room for only 2 as he packs for camp. How many different combinations of 2 books can Michael choose?

_____

5. Two friends meet at a restaurant at 9:00 a.m. on Tuesday. If one returns for a meal every six hours and the other every 8 hours,
  ▶ on which day of the week will they have their next meal together?

_____

  ▶ will their next meal together most likely be eggs, a sandwich, or roast chicken? Why?

_____

_____

6. If 6 friends each shake hands with one another when they meet, how many handshakes will there be in all? (This can be solved exactly the same way as another problem on this page. However, it is disguised to look different. Can you tell which one?)

_____

_____

Name _____

Following a Flowchart

These temperatures were all recorded on the same day:

Albuquerque 87°F, Atlanta 85°F, Austin 94°F,
Baltimore 80°F, Boston 71°F, Casper 82°F, Denver
74°F, El Paso 93°F, Hartford 79°F, Houston 91°F, Key
West 87°F, Little Rock 86°F, Miami 89°F, Omaha
70°F, Philadelphia 81°F, Providence 77°F, Richmond
85°F, St. Louis 80°F, San Antonio 97°F, Seattle 72°F,
Toledo 68°F.

Make a stem and leaf table for the data by following
this flowchart:

Now look at the original data list and the stem and leaf
table you have made. For each question, decide
whether you can answer it and where you would look
to find the answer most easily.

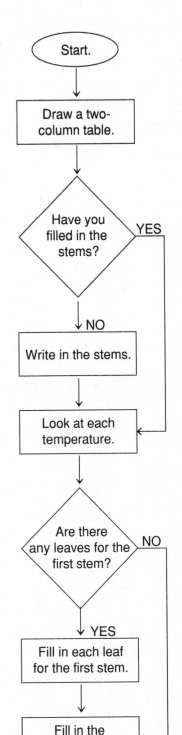

1. Which section of the
country had the warmest
temperatures?

_____

_____

_____

_____

2. What city in the United
States had the warmest
temperature that day?

_____

_____

_____

_____

3. Are more temperatures
in the seventies or
eighties shown?

_____

_____

_____

4. Does the alphabetical
order of the cities have
any relation to their
temperatures?

_____

_____

_____

_____

Population Facts

The table below lists the number of people per square mile in each of the 50 states and Washington, DC as of 1988. These figures are known as population densities.

In order to organize these data into a usable form, consider these questions.

Population Densities (per square mile)

State	Density	State	Density	State	Density	State	Density
Ala	80	Ill.	208	Mon.	6	R.I.	935
Alaska	1	Ind.	154	Neb.	21	S.C.	113
Ariz.	30	Iowa	51	N.H.	118	Tenn.	118
Ark.	46	Kans.	30	N.H.	118	Tenn.	118
Calif.	177	Ky.	94	N.J.	1,027	Tex.	64
Colo.	32	La.	100	N.Mex.	12	Utah	20
Conn.	659	Maine	38	N.Y.	376	Vt.	59
Del.	333	Md.	461	N.C.	131	Va.	149
D.C.	9,873	Mass.	461	N. Dak.	10	Wash.	68
Fla.	222	Mich.	748	Ohio	263	W. Va.	79
Ga.	107	Minn.	162	Okla.	48	Wis.	88
Hawaii	169	Miss.	56	Oreg.	28	Wyo.	5
Ida.	12	Mo.	68	Pa.	266		

1. Does it appear that the data can easily be organized into a stem and leaf table? Why or why not?

_____

2. If your answer to question 1 was no, which densities would prevent a stem and leaf table from being useful?

_____

3. What would be an appropriate frequency interval if you were going to complete a frequency table for all the data?

_____

4. What incorrect impression might you give about Washington, D.C., and New Jersey if your highest interval were "1,000 or more"?

_____

5. What could you do on the frequency table or in a histogram to avoid creating that wrong impression?

_____

6. What would you be able to tell about the total population of each state after making a frequency table and histogram from these data?

_____

To Tell the Truth

Decide if the statements can be true at the same time.

1. Dana is standing next to Bill.
Bob is standing to the right of Dana.
Bob is standing to the right of Bill.

_____

2. Mrs. Le-Bel lives 60 miles from the
southern border of her state. She left her
house and drove 6 hours south on the
freeway. She turned around and drove 2
hours north. She was in her home state

after the 8-hour drive. _____

3. At dawn the temperature was 48° F.
At noon it was 17° warmer. At sunset the
temperature was 13° less than at noon. It
was 4° warmer at sunset than at dawn.

_____

4. Lincoln is between Roseville
and Vacaville.
Vacaville is between Lincoln and Aurora.
Roseville is between Lincoln
and Vacaville.

_____

Decide if the conclusion follows from the given
statements.

5. All dogs are mammals.
All dogs have 4 legs.
All mammals have 4 legs.

_____

6. 13 is a prime number.
Prime numbers have only 2 factors.
1 and 13 are the only factors of 13.

_____

7. Dinosaurs first appeared about 200
million years ago.
Some dinosaurs were carnivorous.
200 million years ago all animals ate
meat.

_____

8. The Dallas Cowboys are a football team.
All football teams have a quarterback.
All quarterbacks are Cowboys.

_____

10. Some artists are sculptors.
Some sculptors learn to weld.
Some welders are sculptors.

_____

9. All eighth graders are expected to
do homework.
Homework is studying outside of class.
All eighth graders study outside of class.

_____

Mean, Median, and Mode Puzzles

Ring the correct solutions to these puzzles.

Puzzle 1

Which three of these nembers have a mean or average of 57?

17   36   52   83

Puzzle 2

Which four of these numbers have a mean of 429?

148   217   412   527   629

Puzzle 3

Which three of these numbers have a mode of 63 and a mean of 71?

41   52   63   63   87

Puzzle 4

Which three of these numbers have a median of 53 and a mean of 50?

19   27   34   53   78

Puzzle 5

Which four of these numbers have a mean the same as the mode?

2.6   4.6   6.2   6.2   9.8

Puzzle 6

Which three of these numbers have a mean the same as the median?

0.7   2.4   3.5   6.3

Puzzle 7

Which three of these numbers have a mean of 15.06?

3.15   31.5   64.2   6.42

72.6   7.26

Puzzle 8

Which five of these numbers have a mode of 6.7, a median of 5.4, and a mean of 5?

1.7   3.6   4.5   5.4   6.7

6.7   9.1

Name _____

Don't Box Me In

1. The students in Mr. Chen's math class decided that they would take part-time jobs for the school year to help pay for a graduation trip. Here are the amounts in dollars earned by the 20 students: 95, 42, 76, 300, 81, 145, 74, 130, 188, 91, 226, 82, 94, 60, 88, 72, 70, 164, 237, 94. Draw a box and whisker graph for this set of data.

2. If each student donates half of his or her savings to a local charity, what would be the new list of data?

_____, _____, _____, _____, _____,

_____, _____, _____, _____, _____,

_____, _____, _____, _____, _____,

_____, _____, _____, _____, _____,

Draw a box and whisker graph for this new set of data.

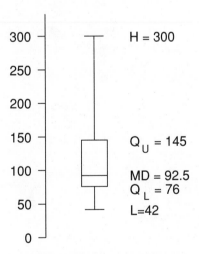

3. Do the diagrams look similar? _____ Explain.

_____

_____

_____

Mean Snowfall

These are annual snowfalls in inches for five cities.

Montreal	Jasper	Murdo	Shelby	Minot
88.4	131.1	79.2	128.6	101.3

Use the above information to answer the questions.
Round your answer to the correct number of
significant digits.

1. What was the mean snowfall for Montreal and Minot? _____

2. What was the mean snowfall for the five cities? _____

3. What was the mean snowfall for Jasper, Murdo,
and Shelby? _____

4. The mean snowfall for which two cities is 109 in.? _____

5. The mean snowfall for which two cities is 105 in.? _____

6. The mean snowfall for which three cities is 103 in.? _____

7. The mean snowfall for which three cities is 103 in.? _____

8. If one more city with an annual snowfall of 111.6 in.
were averaged with the others, by how much would
the mean be raised? _____

Easy to Miss

The problems on this page seem easy. They *are* easy—
easy to miss. You must read each problem carefully in
order to solve it correctly. Ring the best answer for
each problem.

1. Linda bought a T-shirt for $3.00. She
bought a blouse that cost $2.50 more than
the T-shirt. How much did she spend in
all?

A $1.50   **B** $5.50   **C** $8.50

2. A bottle of juice costs $2.15. A loaf of
bread costs $1.10 less than the juice. How
much do the bread and juice cost
together?

A $1.05   **B** $1.10   **C** $3.20

3. Sharon weighs 45.6 kg and Peg weighs
3.8 kg more than Sharon. How much do
Sharon and Peg weigh together?

A 105 kg   **B** 95 kg   **C** 59.4 kg

4. An electronic game and a calculator
together cost $61.40. The electronic game
costs $36.40 more than the calculator.
How much does the calculator cost?

A $12.50   **B** $23.90   **C** $61.40

5. Gary has $0.60 in change. Half of his
coins are nickels and the other half are
dimes. What is the value of his dimes?

A $0.30   **B** $0.40   **C** $0.20

6. It is 50.8 km from Allison to Centerville.
The distance from Centerville to Belltown
is 24.6 km longer than the distance from
Allison to Centerville. How far is it from
Allison to Belltown?

Allison • Centerville
 • •Belltown

A 126.2   **B** 26.2   **C** 75.4

7. Dick has $1.75 in change. Half of the
coins are quarters and the other half are
dimes. What is the value of his dimes?

A $0.80   **B** $0.50   **C** $1.00

8. Neil weighs 30.6 kg while standing on
one foot. How much does he weigh
standing on both feet?

A 61.2 kg   **B** 91.8 kg   **C** 30.6 kg

Ice Cream Algebra

A regular ice cream cone may have a base with a diameter of 2 inches and be 5 inches high. A super cone has a diameter of 4 inches and the same height as a regular cone. How much more ice cream can the super cone hold than the regular?

Make an estimate first. You can use what you know about evaluating algebraic expressions to find the exact answer.

The formula for the volume of a cone is $V = \frac{1}{3}\pi r^2 h$ where r is the radius of the base and h is the height of the cone.

You can evaluate this formula to find the difference in the size of the two cones. The result may surprise you.

Regular	Super
$V = \frac{1}{3} \cdot \frac{22}{7} \cdot 1^2 \cdot 5$	$V = \frac{1}{3} \cdot \frac{22}{7} \cdot 2^2 \cdot 5$
$= \frac{22}{21} \cdot 1 \cdot 5$	$= \frac{22}{21} \cdot 4 \cdot 5$
$= 5.2$ cu in.	$= 20.9$ cu in.

The super cone holds 4 times as much as the regular.

Evaluate these formulas to find what happens to the volume of a figure when the given measurement is changed.

1. Cube: volume = s^3 where s is the length of an edge.
   Cube 1: $s = 5$ cm
   Cube 2: $s = 10$ cm
   Volume is 8 times greater.

2. Cylinder: volume = $\pi r^2 h$ where r is the radius of the base, h the height.
   Cylinder 1: $r = 3$ in., $h = 9$ in.
   Cylinder 2: $r = 6$ in., $h = 9$ in.
   Volume is 4 times greater.

3. Sphere: volume = $\frac{4 \pi r^3}{3}$ where r is the radius of the sphere.
   Sphere 1: $r = 6$ mm
   Sphere 2: $r = 12$ mm
   Volume is 8 times greater.

Interesting Shapes

Estimate the area of each region. Combine partial units
to create whole units where possible.

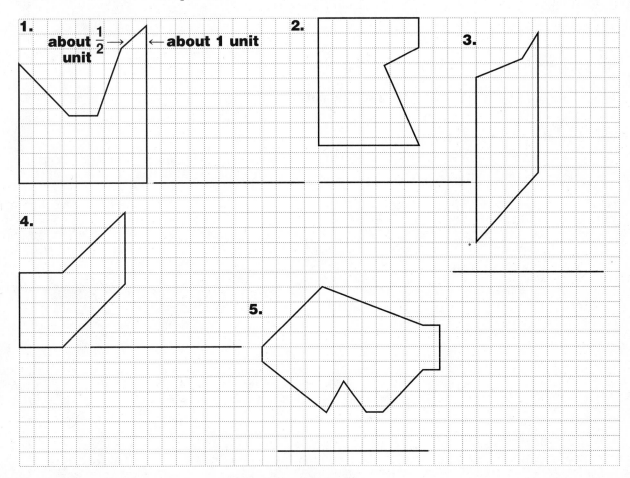

1.
about $\frac{1}{2}$ →
unit ← about 1 unit

2.

3.

4.

5.

6. Draw your initials in block letters in the grid below.
   Calculate the area of the shapes these letters create.

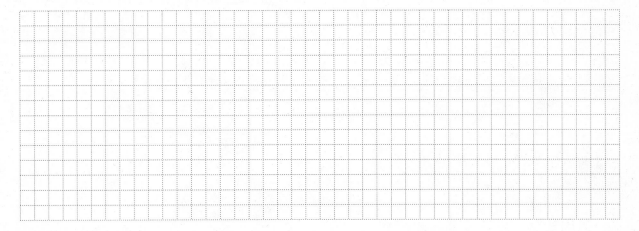

Name _____

Grid Area

This is the way Andrea found the area of the shaded figure.

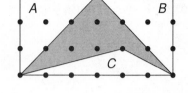

Area of whole grid: $3 \times 6 = 18$ square units

Area of triangle A: $\frac{1}{2} \times 3 \times 3 = 4.5$ square units

Area of triangle B: $\frac{1}{2} \times 3 \times 3 = 4.5$ square units

Area of triangle C: $\frac{1}{2} \times 6 \times 1 = 3$ square units

The total area of A, B, and C = 4.5 + 4.5 + 3 = 12 square units.
The area of the grid – the total area of A, B, and C = 18 – 12 = 6 square units.
The area of the shaded figure is 6 square units.

Find the area of each figure.

1.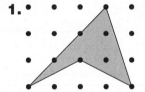

2.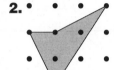

3.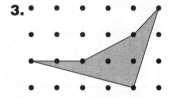

_____

4.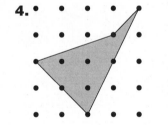

5.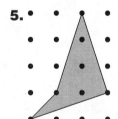

6.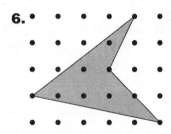

_____

7.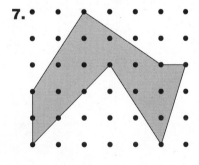

8.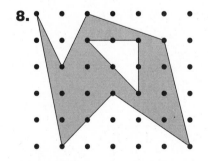

_____

As Far as the Eye Can See

How much of Earth can you see from an airplane? The circles on the map show the land area that can be seen from airplanes flying at different altitudes. Each problem number corresponds to the circle on the map with the same number. Use your calculator to solve these problems.

Area of a Circle
Formula: $a = \pi r^2$
[ON/AC] r $\boxed{\times}$ r $\boxed{\times}$ 3.14 $\boxed{=}$

1. In this airplane you are flying at an altitude of 2 km. How many square kilometers of land can you see?

_____

2. Now you are flying at an altitude of 4 km. How many square kilometers of land can you see?

_____

3. How many square kilometers of land can be seen from an altitude of 8 km?

_____

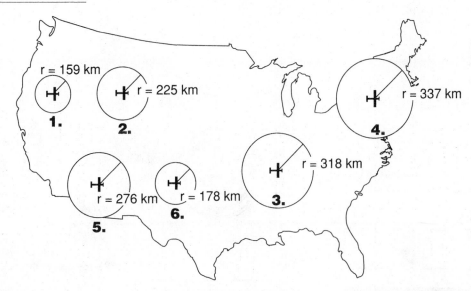

4. What is the area that can be seen from an altitude of 10 km?

_____

5. This airplane is at an altitude of 6 km. How many square kilometers of land can you see?

_____

6. How many square kilometers can be seen from a height of 2.5 km?

_____

7. Flying at a height of 3 km you can see about 195 km in all directions. How many square kilometers of land can be seen from this height?

_____

8. The area of Iowa is 145,830 km². About what percent of Iowa can be seen when flying over the center of the state at an altitude of 3 km?

_____

Name _____

Artsy Algebra

Al-Khowarizmi's Art Gallery, an extremely avant-garde museum, held an exhibit of picture frames. The title of each work of art was going to be a description of the area of each frame. However, as these things sometimes happen, the plaques with the titles got separated from the frames while the exhibit was being set up.

Can you identify which plaque belongs with each work of art?

When you have correctly matched each frame with its title, arrange the letters inside the paintings to spell the branch of mathematics named for the work of the ancient Arabian mathemetician,

Al-Khowarizmi. _____

1. $A = s_1^2 - s_2^2$ _____

2. $A = \frac{1}{2}bh - \pi r^2$ _____

3. $A = \pi r^2 - s^2$ _____

4. $A = \pi r_1^2 - \pi r_2^2$ _____

5. $A = l_1 w_1 - l_2 w_2$ _____

6. $A = lw - (lw + lw)$ _____

7. $A = \frac{1}{2}(b_1 + b_2)h - \frac{1}{2}(b_1 + b_2)h$ _____

Name _____

Too Many Books!

At the Library of Math and Science you can win an almanac by solving the following problems.

Show your work.

1. In the physics section there are 12 more books on the first shelf than there are on the second shelf. If the number of books on the second shelf were doubled and 17 were subtracted, the result would equal the number of books on the first shelf. How many books are on the first two

shelves? _____

_____

_____

_____

_____

2. The biology section has 15 more books than the chemistry section. If the chemistry section had 3 less than twice as many books, it would have the same number of books as the biology section. How many books are in both sections

together? _____

_____

_____

_____

_____

3. The algebra section has 13 more books than the geometry section. The librarian plans to triple the number of books in the geometry section. Then there would be 15 more geometry books than algebra books. How many books will be in these two

sections? _____

_____

_____

_____

_____

Name _____

Polygons to Triangles

The region of any polygon can be divided into triangular regions. Draw segments to divide these polygons into the fewest possible triangles. Write the number of sides of each polygon and the number of triangles.

1.

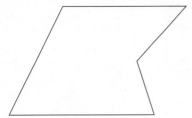

Number of sides: _____

Fewest triangles: _____

2.

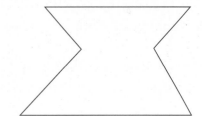

Number of sides: _____

Fewest triangles: _____

3.

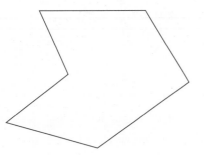

Number of sides: _____

Fewest triangles: _____

4.

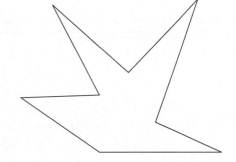

Number of sides: _____

Fewest triangles: _____

5.

Number of sides: _____

Fewest triangles: _____

6.

Number of sides: _____

Fewest triangles: _____

Name _____

Box Areas

Each figure below can be folded to form an open box. Find the length (l) and the width (w) of each face of the box. You may have to mentally fold the box to determine the dimensions of each face. Then find the area of the face and the total area of the box figure.

1.

32 cm

A	B
C	16 cm
D	E	16 cm

Face	l	w	Area
A			
B			
C			
D			
E			
Total			

2.

58 cm

| A | 12 cm |
| B | |
27 cm
| C | D | E |

Face	l	w	Area
A			
B			
C			
D			
E			
Total			

3.

20.5 cm   C

16.2 cm   A   B   D

E

16.2 cm

Face	l	w	Area
A			
B			
C			
D			
E			
Total			

4.

| A | B | 18 cm |
| C | D | 18 cm |
45.6 cm
E

Face	l	w	Area
A			
B			
C			
D			
E			
Total			

Name _____

Surface Area and Volume Experiment

The relationship between volume and surface area is important to an architect planning an office building. Assume you are designing a building consisting of ten offices. Use wooden cubes or sugar cubes to represent the offices and experiment to answer the questions below.

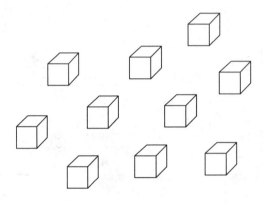

How would you design the building so that it has:

1. An odd number of floors with the same number of offices on each floor?

_____

_____

2. A courtyard?

_____

_____

3. Four sections, each with a different number of levels?

_____

_____

4. The smallest surface area possible (to minimize heating and cooling costs)? What is the smallest possible surface area?

_____

_____

5. The largest number of walls for windows (to maximize the amount of light)? How many walls can have windows?

_____

_____

6. If you were designing this building, would you more likely be guided by your answer to Question 4 or Question 5, or would you choose a compromise? Explain.

_____

_____

Ranking Volumes

All of the containers below are drawn to the same scale. Without doing any computation, rank the containers in order of their volume from the largest to the smallest. Then find the volume of each container and see how they actually rank in volume.

A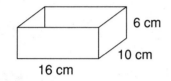
6 cm
10 cm
16 cm

B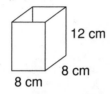
12 cm
8 cm
8 cm

C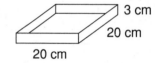
3 cm
20 cm
20 cm

D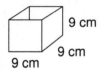
9 cm
9 cm
9 cm

E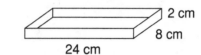
2 cm
8 cm
24 cm

F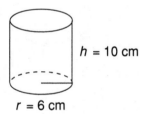
$h = 10$ cm
$r = 6$ cm

G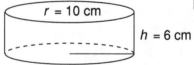
$r = 10$ cm
$h = 6$ cm

H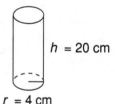
$h = 20$ cm
$r = 4$ cm

Estimated Rank

Rank	Figure
1	
2	
3	
4	
5	
6	
7	
8	

Actual Rank

Rank	Figure	Volume cm^3
1		
2		
3		
4		
5		
6		
7		
8		

Volumes of Volume

Match each figure with the formula for its volume.

1. Prism $V = \frac{1}{3}\pi r^2 h$

2. Pyramid $V = Bh$

3. Cylinder $V = \pi r^2 h$

4. Cone $V = \frac{1}{3}Bh$

Find the volumes. Use 3.14 for π.

5.   **6.**   **7.**

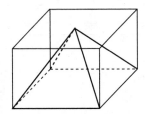   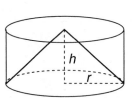   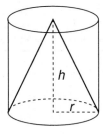

$B = 44$ mm² $r = 3$ cm $r = 9$ cm
$h = 24$ mm $h = 3$ cm $h = 20$ cm

Prism = _____   Cylinder = _____   Cylinder = _____

Pyramid = _____   Cone = _____   Cone = _____

8. In Exercises 5, 6, and 7, what is the relationship between the volumes of the two figures?

_____

9. The cylinder has a diameter of 10 cm.
Find the volume of the cylinder. Find the
volume of the prism.

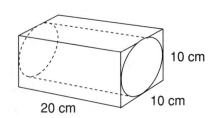

10 cm

20 cm   10 cm

_____   _____

Applied Problem Solving

1. You want to design a shipping box for some cups. Each box should hold 4 cups. List the things you need to consider and the questions you need to answer. Then decide what size and shape your shipping box will be and make a drawing of it.

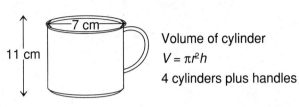

Volume of cylinder

$V = \pi r^2 h$

4 cylinders plus handles

Some things to consider:

_____

_____

_____

Some questions to answer:

_____

_____

_____

Your decision:

_____

_____

_____

2. Judy is buying wallpaper. Her room is 3.5 m wide, 4 m long, and the ceiling is 2.9 m from the floor. There are 2 windows in her room, each 2.1 m high and 1.13 m wide. The door is 2 m high and 0.95 m wide. If she papers the walls and ceiling, what is the surface to be papered?

_____

3. Robert is making square cutting boards with an area of 900 square cm. What is the length of each side of the cutting boards?

_____

Name _____

The Glogs of Nog

On the imaginary island of Nog, money is measured in units called glogs. Here are the weights of the coins.

     1-glog coin = 4 grams

     5-glog coins = 10 grams

     10-glog coins = 12 grams

     25-glog coins = 20 grams

Use the weights of the coins to determine how much money each person has. Some may have more than one amount.

1. Alberto has 14 grams in coins.

_____

2. Matthew has 10 coins weighing a total of 200 grams.

_____

3. Jessica has 40 grams in coins. Use at least 1-glog coin.

_____

4. Misha has 3 coins, weighing a total of 24 grams.

_____

5. Natalie has 2 coins weighing a total of 24 grams.

_____

6. Tyrell has 42 grams in coins.

_____

7. What is the greatest possible weight of 100 glogs?

_____

8. What is the smallest possible weight of 100 glogs?

_____

Solving Problems Mentally

Solve these problems using mental math.

1. Paco is 8 years younger than his brother who is 21. How old is Paco?

   _____

2. Roseanne weighs 11 times as much as her newborn sister. Her sister weighs 9 lb. What does Roseanne weigh?

   _____

3. This week Jacob received 3 times as many phone calls as his father. His father received 7 phone calls. How many phone calls did Jacob receive?

   _____

4. One third of Mrs. Bergen's grocery bill was spent on food for her son's birthday party. She spent $33 on the party. What was her total grocery bill?

   _____

5. One Thursday, the temperature varied 18°C in Denver. If Denver had a high temperature that day of 30°C, what was the low temperature for the day?

   _____

6. Kansas became a state 65 years after Tennessee. Tennessee became a state in 1796. In what year did Kansas become a state?

   _____

7. Rounded to the nearest thousand, Peru is 186,000 km^2 larger than Bolivia. Bolivia is 1,099,000 km^2. What is the area of Peru?

   _____

8. Mona Movie-Star paid 50 times more for her house than Mary Meager-Mortgage. Mona spent $2,500,000 for her house. What did Mary spend?

   _____

A Number of Strategies

Use guess and check to solve.

1. Mr. Boom is three times as old as his daughter. In 9 years he will be twice as old as his daughter. Find the ages now.

   _____

2. The product of two consecutive odd numbers is 783. Find the numbers.

   _____

3. What is the only number you can multiply by itself and get a product of 4,489?

   _____

4. The length of a rectangle is 4 more than the width. The perimeter is 40 meters. Find the length.

   _____

Find a digit for each letter so that each problem is correct. Use guess and check.

5.   A,BCD
    ×   AE
        FCFGH
        EABJ
       ‾‾‾‾‾‾‾
       BE,JEH

   Hint: H = 0

6.
   $$\begin{array}{r} \text{VZT} \\ \text{WX}\overline{)\text{WZ,YTS}} \\ \underline{\text{WZY}} \\ \text{TS} \\ \underline{\text{TS}} \end{array}$$

   _____

7. These digits are written in a definite order.

   8 5 4 9 1 7 6 3 2 0

   Can you figure it out?

   _____

   _____

Opposites Attract

In each of the following, describe an inverse operation.

1. Multiplying by 2

_____

2. Subtracting 43

_____

3. Walking up 6 flights of stairs

_____

4. Gaining 4 kilograms

_____

5. A temperature drop of 7°C

_____

_____

6. A bank withdrawal of $342.91

_____

8. Changing your recipe to make $\frac{1}{3}$ as many cookies

_____

7. A salary cut of $1,000 per year

_____

9. Running the New York Marathon 3 times slower than the first-place winner

_____

10. Finding a shirt at a discount store for $5 below retail

_____

_____

11. Reducing your gasoline consumption by 8 miles per gallon

_____

_____

12. Improving your typing by 10 words per minute

_____

_____

13. Sleeping 2 hours more each night

_____

14. Increasing your driving speed by 4 miles per hour

_____

One-Step Inequalities

The steps used to solve an equation can be used to
solve an addition or subtraction **inequality**.

Examples:

A number plus 8 is less than 21.
How great is the number?

$$n + 8 < 21$$
$$n + 8 - 8 < 21 - 8 \leftarrow$$
$$n < 13$$

The number is less than 13.

*Add or subtract the
same number from
each side of the
inequality.*

A number times 5 is less than 45.
How great is the number?

$$5y < 45$$
$$\frac{5y}{5} < \frac{45}{5}$$
$$y < 9$$

The number is less than 9.

Solve these inequalities.

1. $x - 7 > 23$

_____

_____

2. $\frac{t}{3} > 7$

_____

_____

3. $m - 9 < 3$

_____

_____

4. $p + 10 > 20$

_____

_____

5. $\frac{d}{5} > 10$

_____

_____

6. $46 + t < 57$

_____

_____

7. $y - 15 > 19$

_____

_____

8. $20y < 40$

_____

_____

9. $f - 23 < 5$

_____

_____

10. $j + 29 > 30$

_____

_____

11. $\frac{m}{3} < 23$

_____

_____

12. $16 + x < 33$

_____

_____

13. $z - 24 < 55$

_____

_____

14. $\frac{b}{5} < 40$

_____

_____

15. $d + 84 < 99$

_____

_____

Name _____

Deliver the Results

Use these tables to answer the questions.

Parcel Post Rate Schedule

1 lb not exceeding	Local	1 & 2	Zones 3	4	5	6	7	8
2	$1.52	$1.55	$1.61	$1.70	$1.83	$1.99	$2.15	$2.48
3	1.58	1.63	1.73	1.86	2.06	2.30	2.55	3.05
4	1.65	1.71	1.84	2.02	2.29	2.61	2.94	3.60
5	1.71	1.79	1.96	2.18	2.52	2.92	3.32	4.07
6	1.78	1.87	2.07	2.33	2.74	3.14	3.64	4.54
7	1.84	1.95	2.18	2.49	2.89	3.38	3.95	5.02
8	1.91	2.03	2.30	2.64	3.06	3.63	4.27	5.55
9	1.97	2.11	2.41	2.75	3.25	3.93	4.63	6.08
10	2.04	2.19	2.52	2.87	3.46	4.22	5.00	6.62
11	2.10	2.28	2.60	3.00	3.68	4.51	5.38	7.15
12	2.17	2.36	2.66	3.10	3.89	4.80	5.75	7.69

Fourth Class Rate Schedule

Weight lb	Local	1&2	Zones 3	4	5	6	7	8
1.5	$0.69	$0.92	$0.94	$0.97	$1.02	$1.08	$1.16	$1.19
2	0.69	0.93	0.95	0.99	1.06	1.14	1.25	1.28
2.5	0.69	0.93	0.96	1.01	1.10	1.20	1.33	1.38
3	0.69	0.94	0.97	1.03	1.14	1.25	1.41	1.47
3.5	0.69	0.94	0.98	1.05	1.17	1.31	1.50	1.56
4	0.69	0.95	0.99	1.07	1.21	1.37	1.58	1.66
4.5	0.69	0.95	1.00	1.09	1.25	1.42	1.67	1.75
5	0.70	0.96	1.02	1.12	1.29	1.48	1.75	1.85

Priority Mail Rate Schedule

Weight To 1 lb	Zones 1,2,3	4	5	6
	$2.24	$2.24	$2.24	$2.34
1.5	2.30	2.42	2.56	2.72
2	2.54	2.70	2.88	3.09
2.5	2.78	2.96	3.21	3.47
3	3.01	3.25	3.53	3.85
3.5	3.25	3.53	3.85	4.22
4	3.49	3.81	4.18	4.60
4.5	3.73	4.09	4.50	4.97
5	3.97	4.37	4.83	5.35

1. Harriet is mailing a book weighing 3.5 pounds to a friend in zone 6. What will it cost to mail the book fourth class?

_____

2. Randy is mailing a book weighing 2.3 pounds to his sister in zone 7. How much more will it cost to mail the book parcel post than fourth class?

_____

3. Tina is mailing a 6-pound 5-ounce package to zone 3 and an 8-pound 3-ounce package to zone 8. How much will it cost to mail them both parcel post?

_____

4. Phan is mailing a package weighing 4.8 pounds to zone 2. How much more will it cost to mail it priority than parcel post?

_____

5. Jeanette has two packages to mail, one weighing 11 pounds 9 ounces, the other weighing 6 pounds 3 ounces. How much will it cost to mail both parcel post to zone 5?

_____

6. Betsy is mailing two packages to zone 4. One weighs 6.5 pounds and the other weighs 9.8 pounds. How much will it cost to mail them parcel post?

_____

Using Critical Thinking

Cal the the caveman likes to go in and out of caves. One day his friend Gog said, "If you start outside my cave, you can come into my cave and stay for dinner if when you walk in the room the number of times you have passed through the door is **even**. You may pass in and out of the door as many times as you like."

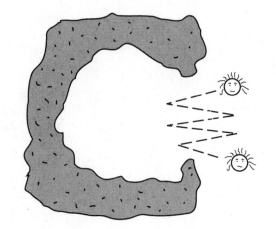

Does Cal get to stay for dinner at Gog's cave? _____

Use the diagram at right to help complete the table.

Number of times Cal Passed Through the Door	Odd or Even Number	Inside or Outside
1	odd	inside
2		
5		
54		
1,067		
8,888		
906,400		
1,021,323		

Cal had an idea. He told Gog, "You must start inside your cave. You cannot come out to find food for dinner unless you walk out your door an **even** number of times. You may go in and out as many times as you like."

If Gog did what Cal said would he be able to come out to find food for dinner? _____

How many times would Gog have to pass through the cave door if Cal let him come out on an odd number of passes? _____

Name _____

Variables and Expressions

Evaluate these expressions. Substitute 12 for each variable.

1. $2w$ **2.** $7 + x$ **3.** $c - 3$ **4.** $\frac{t}{2}$ **5.** $3n - 1$

_____ _____ _____ _____ _____

Evaluate these expressions. Substitute 9 for each variable.

6. $2x + 3$ **7.** $\frac{18}{m} + 4$ **8.** $\frac{r - 1}{2}$ **9.** $3(s + 1)$ **10.** $23 - 2w$

_____ _____ _____ _____ _____

Evaluate these expressions. Substitute 20 for each variable.

11. $2p - 10$ **12.** $4(c - 2)$ **13.** $\frac{3 + m}{2}$ **14.** $\frac{35 - t}{2}$ **15.** $\frac{4n}{5}$

_____ _____ _____ _____ _____

Write three expressions equal to 15. Give the value of each variable.

16. _____ **17.** _____ **18.** _____

$t =$ _____ $m =$ _____ $w =$ _____

Write three expressions equal to 3. Give the value of each variable.

19. _____ **20.** _____ **21.** _____

$x =$ _____ $c =$ _____ $r =$ _____

Name _____

Equations That Balance

Find the missing weights by writing and solving an
equation for each problem.

Example: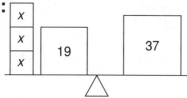

$$3x + 19 = 37$$
$$3x + 19 - 19 = 37 - 19$$
$$x = \frac{18}{3}$$
$$x = 6$$

1.

$w =$ _____

2.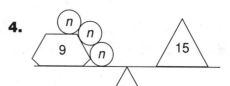

$n =$ _____

3.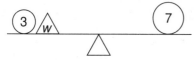

$x =$ _____

4.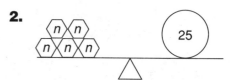

$n =$ _____

5.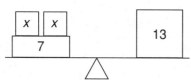

$n =$ _____

6.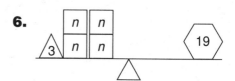

$n =$ _____

7.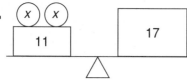

$x =$ _____

8.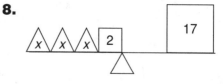

$x =$ _____

9.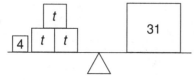

$t =$ _____

10.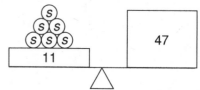

$s =$ _____

Name _____

Keeping the Balance

The steps used to solve equations can be used to solve inequalities.

Examples

A number plus 8 is less than 21. How great is the number?

A number minus 4 is greater than 15. How great is the number?

$$n + 8 < 21$$
$$n + 8 - 8 < 21 - 8$$
$$n < 13$$

Add or subtract the same number from each side of the inequality.

$$x - 4 > 15$$
$$x - 4 + 4 > 15 + 4$$
$$x > 19$$

The number is less than 13.

The number is greater than 19.

A number times 5 is less than 45. How great is the number?

$$5y < 45$$
$$\frac{5y}{5} < \frac{45}{5}$$
$$y < 9$$

A number divided by 11 is greater than 4. How great is the number?

$$\frac{n}{11} > 4$$
$$11 \times \frac{n}{11} > 4 \times 11$$
$$n > 44$$

The number is less than 9.

The number is greater than 44.

Solve these inequalities.

1. $x - 7 > 23$

2. $r + 5 < 18$

3. $m - 9 < 3$

4. $\frac{w}{3} < 1$

5. $\frac{d}{5} > 10$

6. $9f < 81$

Name _____

Using Functions

Complete each table for the given function.

1. $m = \dfrac{(7+y)}{2} + 10$

y	3	7	9	11	21
m					

2. $r = 4p - 9$

p	3	6	12	18	24
r					

3. $v = \dfrac{d}{3} - 1$

v					
d	12	24	33	60	93

4. $c = 5(s - 2)$

c					
s	4	5	9	14	17

5. $f = \dfrac{c}{n} - 1$

c	10	100	51	5,000
n	2	5	17	10
f				

6. $t = qk$

q	7	10	36	800
k	9	4	2	60
t				

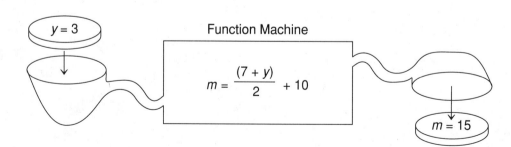

Function Machine

$y = 3$

$m = \dfrac{(7 + y)}{2} + 10$

$m = 15$

Function Problems

Make a function table for the following situations.

1. In the spring we set our clocks ahead 1 hour. This function shows what the winter time becomes.

$f(w) = w + 1$

w	f(w)
2:00	_____
5:00	_____
8:00	_____
12:00	_____

2. Mrs. Goldman's oven temperature is always 100° hotter than what it is set for. What is the real oven temperature?

$f(t) = t + 100$

t	f(t)
200°	_____
300°	_____
375°	_____
425°	_____

3. In the fall of his 8th-grade year, Justin realizes that he will graduate from high school in $4\frac{1}{2}$ years. What is his graduation year, based on the year he will be an 8th grader? $f(y) = y + 4\frac{1}{2}$

y	f(y)
1990	_____
1992	_____
1997	_____
2003	_____

4. Many states have a 5% sales tax. To calculate a total sales bill, add 5% of the price to the original price.

$f(p) = p + 0.05n$

p	f(p)
$5.00	_____
$12.00	_____
$25.00	_____
$100.00	_____

Symmetric Designs

Plot each (x,y) pair on the graph below. Point A is found
by moving 24 to the right, then moving up 12. Connect
point A to point B, then B to C, then C to D, and so on.
Finally, connect point L to point A to complete the design.

	A	B	C	D	E	F	G	H	I	J	K	L
x	24	10	12	0	14	12	0	14	12	24	10	12
y	12	18	0	12	6	24	12	18	0	12	6	24

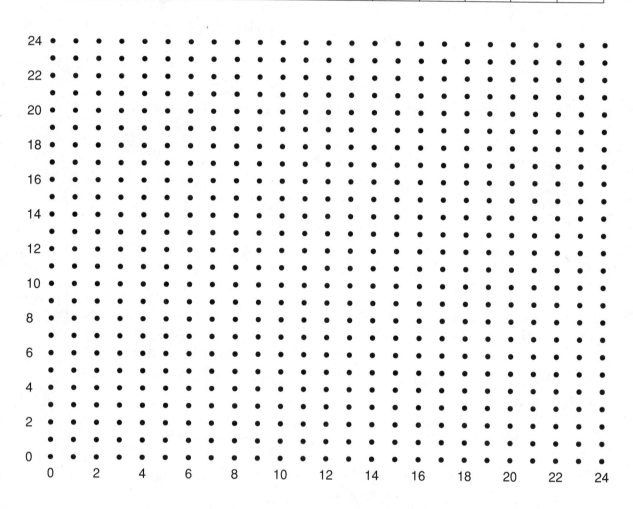

How many lines of symmetry does the completed
figure have?

_____

Exponent Search

Write each of these numbers as the sum or difference of
no more than three square numbers. Some can be written
in more than one way.

1. 5 _____ $2^2 + 1^2$ _____

2. 7 _____ $2^2 + 2^2 - 1^2$ _____

3. 8 _____

4. 10 _____

5. 14 _____

6. 35 _____

7. 22 _____

8. 42 _____

9. 50 _____

10. 27 _____

11. 64 _____

12. 72 _____

13. 52 _____

14. 29 _____

15. 63 _____

16. 75 _____

17. 82 _____

18. 93 _____

Can you write the rest of the numbers between
0 and 100 using exponents? Try it.

It Is Absolutely True or False

Tell which of the following statements are true and which are false.

1. $|8| < |6|$ _____

2. $|2| = 2$ _____

3. $|65| = {}^-65$ _____

4. $|{}^-29| < 29$ _____

5. $|{}^-6.84| \geq 6.84$ _____

6. $|{}^-12| - |{}^-9| \leq 3$ _____

7. $|{}^-6\frac{4}{5}| > \frac{34}{5}$ _____

8. $|9-5| < |9| - |5|$ _____

9. Write an integer that would indicate a 17-yard loss on a football play.   _____

10. Write an integer that indicates 5 seconds before a rocket take-off.   _____

11. Find the opposite of the opposite of 35.   _____

12. Write an integer to express the depth that the abalone is found if it is found 20 feet below sea level.   _____

13. Find the opposite of the opposite of the opposite of 45.   _____

14. Write an integer to indicate a check that bounces for $500.   _____

Find a pattern. Then fill in the blanks.

15.	${}^-9$	${}^-8$			${}^-5$		${}^-3$		${}^-1$	
16.	${}^-15$		${}^-9$	${}^-6$				6		12
17.	36		18		0	${}^-9$			${}^-36$	${}^-45$
18.	1		3	${}^-4$	5			${}^-8$	9	
19.	18	17	${}^-16$		14		${}^-12$	${}^-11$		

Addition of Integers

Use the given numbers to make each equation true.

3	5	7	⁻3	⁻5	⁻7

1. _____ + _____ = ⁻4   **2.** _____ + _____ = 8

3. _____ + _____ = 2   **4.** _____ + _____ = 4

5. _____ + _____ = ⁻12   **6.** _____ + _____ = ⁻2

7. _____ + _____ = 12   **8.** _____ + _____ = 10

9. _____ + _____ = ⁻8   **10.** _____ + _____ = ⁻10

2	6	9	⁻2	⁻6	⁻9

11. _____ + _____ = ⁻11   **12.** _____ + _____ = ⁻7

13. _____ + _____ = 4   **14.** _____ + _____ = ⁻4

15. _____ + _____ = 15   **16.** _____ + _____ = ⁻15

17. _____ + _____ = ⁻8   **18.** _____ + _____ = 7

19. _____ + _____ = 3   **20.** _____ + _____ = 11

21. _____ + _____ = 8   **22.** _____ + _____ = ⁻3

Make eight different addition equations using the given
numbers for the addends. Then find each sum.

3	4	8	⁻3	⁻4	⁻8

23. _____ + _____ = _____   **24.** _____ + _____ = _____

25. _____ + _____ = _____   **26.** _____ + _____ = _____

27. _____ + _____ = _____   **28.** _____ + _____ = _____

29. _____ + _____ = _____   **30.** _____ + _____ = _____

Subtraction Reaction

► Pick a number from Card A and subtract it from a number on Card B. Write your numbers and answer in the column on the right.

► Put an X on your answer on the game board

► Pick two more numbers and try again. The object is to get four answers in a line on the game board in as few tries as possible.

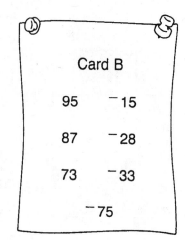

Card A

37	⁻18
26	⁻32
15	⁻46

Card B

95	⁻15
87	⁻28
73	⁻33
	⁻75

Game board:

	⁻59			⁻43	
	31	61	⁻70	80	
58	141	⁻65	105	17	47
⁻43	⁻10	⁻30	3	50	18
127	58	4	133	⁻52	72
113	⁻15	69	⁻54	91	58
	⁻41	⁻1	⁻48	13	
	⁻101	36	⁻90	⁻112	
	⁻43	⁻57	119	⁻29	

1. _____ − _____ = _____

2. _____ − _____ = _____

3. _____ − _____ = _____

4. _____ − _____ = _____

5. _____ − _____ = _____

6. _____ − _____ = _____

7. _____ − _____ = _____

8. _____ − _____ = _____

9. _____ − _____ = _____

10. _____ − _____ = _____

11. _____ − _____ = _____

12. _____ − _____ = _____

13. _____ − _____ = _____

14. _____ − _____ = _____

15. _____ − _____ = _____

Scores

Superior:	Good:	Need practice:
4 to 8 trials	9 to 14	15 or more

Name _____

Think Positively or Negatively

Use what you know about positive and negative
integers to tell whether each statement is **always true**,
sometimes true or **never true**.

a is a positive integer b is a negative integer

1. $(a \div b) \cdot (a \div b) > 0$ _____

2. $a + b > b$ and $a + b < a$ _____

3. $a \cdot b < a$ and $b \cdot a > b$ _____

4. $a^2 > b^2$ _____

5. $(a \div b) \cdot (a \cdot b) > 0$ _____

Write three statements of your own using a and b. Tell
whether they are sometimes, always, or never true.

6. _____

_____

7. _____

_____

8. _____

_____

Think Positive or Negative

The product of two positive integers is positive.

$8 \times 6 = 48$

The product of two negative integers is positive.

$(^-8)(^-6) = 48$

The product of a positive and a negative integers negative.

$(^-8)(6) = ^-48$

When multiplying many negative integers, it can be confusing to figure out if your answer is negative or positive.

Try it this way.

1. Multiply all the numbers without regard to sign.

2. Then count the number of negative integers that were in the group you multiplied.

3. If the **number** of negative integers is even, your answer is positive.

   If the **number** of negative integers is odd, your answer is negative.

Multiply all the numbers.

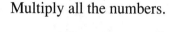
Multiply all the numbers.

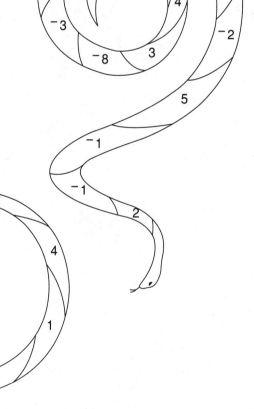

Name _____

Equations and Mental Math

Write one addition equation and one subtraction equation
for the givin solution.

1.

$n = {}^-8$

_____

_____

2.

$y = {}^-10$

_____

_____

Write one multiplication equation and on division
equation for the given solution.

3.

$x = {}^-3$

_____

_____

4.

$r = {}^-12$

_____

_____

Write a number in each box so that the given solution is correct.

5. $\boxed{} \; y = {}^-32$

$y = {}^-8$

6. $m - \boxed{} = 26$

$m = {}^-3$

7. $\dfrac{p}{\boxed{}} = {}^-12$

$p = {}^-48$

8. $\boxed{} \; g = 20$

$g = {}^-4$

9. $w - \boxed{} = 36$

$w = {}^-11$

10. $\boxed{} \; f = {}^-36$

$f = 2$

11. $\dfrac{\boxed{}}{k} = {}^-12$

$k = {}^-7$

12. $\dfrac{\boxed{}}{b} = {}^-12$

$b = {}^-20$

13. $\boxed{} + a = {}^-6$

$a = 17$

Start with the Solution

Write one addition equation and one subtraction equation for the given solution.

1.
$$n = {}^-8$$

_____

_____

2.
$$y = {}^-10$$

_____

_____

Write one multiplication equation and one division equation for the given solution.

3.
$$x = {}^-3$$

_____

_____

4.
$$r = {}^-12$$

_____

_____

Write a number in each box so that the given solution is correct.

5. $\boxed{}\, y = {}^-32$
$$y = {}^-8$$

6. $m - \boxed{} = 26$
$$m = {}^-3$$

7. $\dfrac{p}{\boxed{}} = {}^-12$
$$p = {}^-48$$

8. $\boxed{}\, g = 20$
$$g = {}^-4$$

9. $w - \boxed{} = 36$
$$w = {}^-11$$

10. $\boxed{}\, f = {}^-36$
$$f = {}^-2$$

11. $\dfrac{\boxed{}}{k} = 4$
$$k = {}^-7$$

12. $\dfrac{\boxed{}}{b} = {}^-4$
$$b = {}^-20$$

13. $\boxed{} + a = {}^-6$
$$a = 17$$

Name _____

Calculator Two-Step

Use a calculator to solve the equations.

Example: $9x - 117 = 819$ Check: $9\ \boxed{\times}\ 104\ \boxed{-}\ 117\ \boxed{=}\ 819$
$9x - 117 + 117 = 819 + 117$
$9x = 936$
$x = 104$

1. $13n + 42 = 120$

$n =$ _____

2. $^-42d + {}^-12 = {}^-642$

$d =$ _____

3. $24a - 18 = 174$

$a =$ _____

4. $12t + 35 = 311$

$t =$ _____

5. $15m + 75 = {}^-195$

$m =$ _____

6. $11p - 48 = 95$

$p =$ _____

7. $^-35t + 36 = {}^-139$

$t =$ _____

8. $9r - 61 = {}^+16$

$r =$ _____

9. $^-14x - 57 = {}^-155$

$x =$ _____

10. $23k + 41 = 409$

$k =$ _____

11. $^-17t + 42 = {}^-502$

$t =$ _____

12. $^-31w + 73 = {}^-454$

$w =$ _____

13. $^-12x + {}^-48 = {}^-144$

$x =$ _____

14. $^-12m + {}^-15 = {}^-87$

$m =$ _____

15. $17p + {}^-112 = {}^-44$

$p =$ _____

16. $4y + {}^-18 = 130$

$y =$ _____

17. $54b - 418 = 932$

$b =$ _____

18. $^-78e + 528 = {}^-1,968$

$e =$ _____

Use the Clues

Write and solve an equation for each secret number clue.

1.

> **John's Clue**
> If 8 is subtracted from my number, the result is ⁻6.

_____

_____

2.

> **Carlo's Clue**
> If you multiply my number by ⁻7, the product is 56.

_____

_____

3.

> **Ginny's Clue**
> When 14 is added to my secret number, the result is 5.

_____

_____

4.

> **Chen's Clue**
> If you divide my number by ⁻12, the quotient is equal to ⁻5.

_____

_____

5.

> **Lisa's Clue**
> If the opposite of 16 is added to my number, the sum will be ⁻5.

_____

_____

6.

> **Duane's Clue**
> I subtracted ⁻12 from my secret number and got an answer of 8.

_____

_____

Write your own secret number clues.
Then write and solve equations to find the secret numbers.

7.

> _____Clue

_____

8.

> _____Clue

_____

Symmetric Designs

A symmetric design can be made by placing numbers on a grid in a
pattern. Look for the pattern in the coordinates in the table below.
Plot the points on the grid. Connect the points by drawing lines. Draw
a line between the last point and first point to complete the design.

1. (0, 12)	**2.** (⁻12, 0)	**3.** (0, 6)	**4.** (12, 0)	**5.** (0, ⁻6)	**6.** (⁻12, 0)
7. (0, ⁻12)	**8.** (⁻2, 0)	**9.** (0, 12)	**10.** (2, 0)	**11.** (0, ⁻12)	**12.** (12, 0)

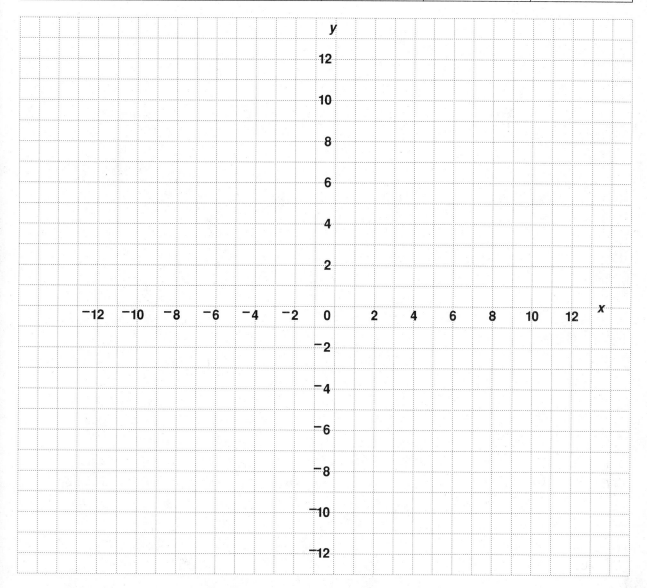

On a sheet of graph paper, make your own table of coordinates.
Try to make a symmetric design. Plot your coordinates on the grid.

Name _____

Testing Solutions

For each of the following equations, decide whether or not the ordered pair is a solution. Write **yes** or **no**. If the answer is no, find the correct y for the given x.

1. $y = 3x$ (3, 9) _____

2. $y = 2x$ (6, 3) _____

3. $y = {}^-x$ (2, 2) _____

4. $y = x + 2$ (4, 6) _____

5. $y = {}^-2x$ (5, ${}^-10$) _____

6. $y = 2 - x$ (3, ${}^-1$) _____

7. $y = 2x - 1$ (${}^-3$, ${}^-7$) _____

8. $y = 3x - 1$ (1, 0) _____

9. $y = x - 4$ (4, 0) _____

10. $y = 5x - 2$ (1, ${}^-3$) _____

11. $y = x - 7$ (2, ${}^-5$) _____

12. $y = x - 5$ (0, 5) _____

13. $y = 9 - x$ (6, 3) _____

14. $y = 9 + x$ (2, 11) _____

15. $y = {}^-2x + 4$ (${}^-3$, ${}^-2$) _____

16. $y = \dfrac{3x}{2} - 2$ (0, ${}^-2$) _____

17. $y = 10 - 3x$ (2, 4) _____

18. $y = 8x$ (0, 0) _____

19. $y = 3x - 5 + 2$ (1, 0) _____

20. $y = 2x + 1$ (${}^-3$, 7) _____

21. $y = 3x - 2$ (${}^-1$, ${}^-1$) _____

22. $y = 3 - 2x$ (${}^-2$, 7) _____

Name _____

Similar Functions

1. Choose any *x* values and find the corresponding y values for the following functions. Graph all of the funtions on the same grid.

$x + y = 5$

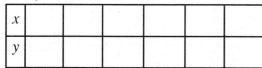

$x + y = 8$

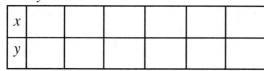

$x + y = 0$

x						
y						

$x + y = -1$

x						
y						

What do you notice? _____

_____

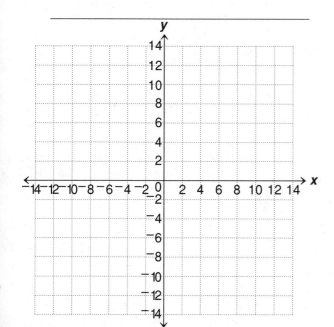

2. Choose any *x* values and find the corresponding y values for the following functions. Graph all of the funtions on the same grid.

$x - y = 2$

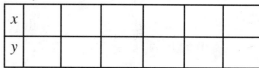

$x - y = 0$

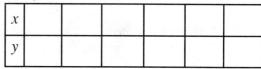

$x - y = 4$

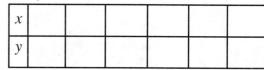

$x - y = -2$

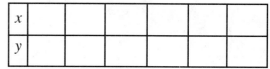

What do you notice? _____

_____

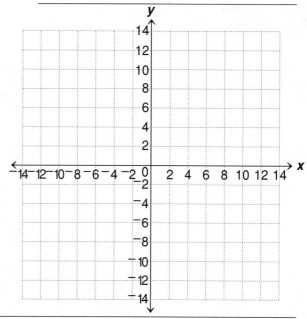

In Vest

Fred is having a difficult time choosing a vest. Below are the choices listed in a catalog.

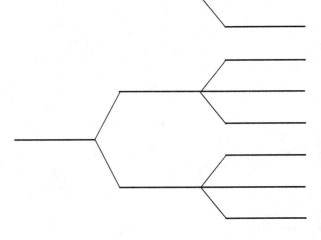

Color: brown, black, green
Style: plain, plaid
Fabric: wool, nylon, cotton

1. Fill in the tree diagram to show all of the possible choices.

2. How many possible choices are there?

_____

3. How many of the possible vest choices are

black? _____

nylon, plain? _____

brown, plaid? _____

brown wool, plain? _____

green cotton? _____

yellow? _____

4. Write one of the following phrases in the blank to make the sentence true.

are green   are cotton

plain   are wool

Half of the possible choices are

_____

Memories Are Made of This

The multiples of 5 are 5, 10, 15, 20, 25, 30, . . .
If you look at these numbers, you may also notice that for each new multiple 5 was added to the number before it.

▶Put 5 into the memory.

▶Press ⬚+ ⬚MR ⬚= to find the next multiple.

▶Press ⬚= again to find the next.

Use your calculator to find the first 20 multiples of each number.

1. 5 _____, _____, _____, _____, _____, _____, _____, _____, _____, _____,

_____, _____, _____, _____, _____, _____, _____, _____, _____

2. 3 _____, _____, _____, _____, _____, _____, _____, _____, _____, _____,

_____, _____, _____, _____, _____, _____, _____, _____, _____

3. 7 _____, _____, _____, _____, _____, _____, _____, _____, _____, _____,

_____, _____, _____, _____, _____, _____, _____, _____, _____

The factors of 30 are 1, 2, 3, 5, 6, 10, 15, 30.
They can be grouped into pairs: $1 \times 30 = 30$, $2 \times 15 = 30$, $3 \times 10 = 30$, $5 \times 6 = 30$.

▶Put 24 into the memory.

▶Press ⬚MR ⬚÷ ⬚1 ⬚= . 1 is the factor paired with 24.

▶ Divide the memory by 2, then by 3, 4, 5, . . . until you have found all of the factors of 24.
(Some of the numbers will not divide evenly. These are not factors of 24.)

Use your calculator to find all of the factors of these numbers.

4. 24 _____

5. 32 _____

6. 44 _____

7. 60 _____

The Great Divide

Dear Family,
    Help your eighth grader to understand some of the applications of divisibility. Sharing things is one possibility.

Answer the following questions.

How many people live in your household right now? _____

If you had won the following quantities of money on a television quiz show, could the members of your family share the winnings evenly? (Each member receives only whole dollars, no cents.)

1. $100

2. $3,000

3. $6,300

_____

_____

_____

4. $1,573

5. $1,245

6. $3,154

_____

_____

_____

If everyone in your household could donate an equal amount of money to buy these items, could the cost be split equally? (Each member donates only dollars, no cents.)

7. television, $400

8. refrigerator, $1,197

_____

_____

9. car, $12,167

10. parrot, $840

_____

_____

Test Your Memory

Calculators can be helpful for determining whether certain
numbers are prime or composite.

Let's test 133.

▶ Store 133 in the memory.

▶ Press MR ÷ 2 = . Then divide by 3, 4, 5, 6, . . .

1. If 133 is not divisible by 3, do you think it will be

divisible by multiples of 3? _____

▶ You really have to divide only by prime numbers less than 133.

2. Does 133 have any factors besides 1 and 133? _____

▶ 7 and 19 are factors of 133.

▶ As soon as you find one factor of a number, you can stop,
because you know that your number is composite.

▶ Use your calculator to determine if 53 is prime or composite.

3. Do you have to divide by every prime number from 2 to 53? _____

▶ As soon as the result given when you press = is less than the
factor you tested, you will know if 53 is prime or composite.

Use your calculator to test the following numbers.
Write **prime** or **composite** for each.

4. 83 _____

5. 117 _____

6. 211 _____

7. 757 _____

8. 557 _____

9. 203 _____

10. 101 _____

11. 657 _____

12. 5,983 _____

Name _____

Minimum-Maximum

When you multiply the least 1-digit whole number by
itself, how many digits are in the answer?

    0 x 0 = 0   1-digit answer

When you multiply the greatest 1-digit whole number
by itself, how many digits are in the answer?

    9 x 9 = 81   2-digit answer

Use your calculator and mental math to complete the chart.
Look for patterns.

Number of Digits in First Factor	Number of Digits in Second Factor	Least Product	Number of Digits in Least Product	Greatest Product	Number of Digits in Greatest Product
1	1	0 x 0 = 0	1	9 x 9 = 81	2
2	2	10 x 10 = 100	3	99 x 99 = 9,801	4
3	3				
4	4				
5	5				
6	6				
2	3	10 x 100 = 1,000		99 x 999 = 98,901	
2	4				
2	5				
3	4				
3	5				
4	7				

Name _____

Prime Time

Prime factorization can be used to check the number
of factors for any number. Follow the steps.

 | Find the prime factors.
90 = 2 x 3 x 3 x 5

  | Write the prime factors with exponents.
$2^1 \times 3^2 \times 5^1$

3 | Add 1 to each exponent and find the
product of the sums.
$(1 + 1) \times (2 + 1) \times (1 + 1) = 2 \times 3 \times 2 = 12$

The number of factors of 90 is 12. ‹

Factors of 90: 1, 2, 3, 5, 6, 9, 10, 15, 18, 30, 45, 90 ‹

> 12 factors
> It checks.

Complete the table.

	Number	Prime factors	Prime factors with exponents	Number of factors	Factors
1.	24	$2 \times 2 \times 2 \times 3$	$2^3 \times 3^1$	$(3 + 1) \times (1 + 1) = 8$	
2.	45				
3.	100				
4.	36				
5.	80				
6.	200				
7.	216				
8.	147				

Strategic Planning

Solve. Use any problem solving strategy.

1. Sam delivers 108 newspapers a week. Some of his customers get a newspaper every day. Ten customers get only a Sunday paper. How many customers get the newspaper every day?

_____

2. Mary made a design by arranging 6 pegs equally spaced around a circle and then connecting each peg to every other peg. How many connecting lines were there?

_____

3. Mark plans to save $1 the first day, $2 the second day, $4 the third day, $8 the fourth day, and so on. How much money will he have saved in 10 days?

_____

4. Barry wants to go to the grocery store, the bookstore, the cleaners, the toy shop, and the park. How many different ways can he do this if he goes to the park first and to the grocery store last?

_____

5. Over the last 8 years, Barbara has averaged $826 in car expenses. This year her car expenses were $988. What is her new average yearly car expense for 9 years?

_____

Clue Me In

Holmes and Watson needed to find the combination to
unlock a locker at Charring Cross Station. Here are the
clues they had.

1. One number is the GCF of 12 and 15.

_____

Factors of 12

4

2   1

12   3

6   15

5

Factors of 15

Common Factors

2. Another number is the GCF of 19 and 57.

_____

3. The third number is the GCF of 27, 36, and 45.

_____

To put the numbers in the proper order, Holmes and
Watson had one more clue.

4. The first number is the square of the third.

Combination: _____ _____ _____

Write your own lock combination problem and clues
to share with Holmes or a friend.

5. _____

_____

_____

Prize Time

A video store is offering prizes, including free cassette rentals, free video cassettes, and a free VCR. To win you must follow these rules.

Every 5th customer gets a red ticket.
Every 7th customer gets a blue ticket.
Every 13th customer gets a green ticket.
Every 14th customer gets a yellow ticket.

You cannot share or pool tickets.

1. To win a free rental you must have both red and blue tickets. Which customer will be the

first to win a free rental? _____

2. To win a cassette you must have red, yellow, and blue tickets. Which customer will be the

first to win a cassette? _____

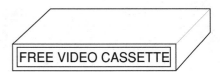

FREE VIDEO CASSETTE

3. To win a VCR you must have red, yellow, green, and blue tickets. Which customer will

be the first to win a VCR? _____

FREE VCR

4. If you and 2 friends *could* pool tickets, which customers should you try to be to win

a VCR most quickly? _____

5. Change the rules to make it faster to win the VCR. You still must use a prime number

greater than 7 for the green ticket. _____

_____

Follow the Plot

Complete the tables by using your calculator to
evaluate each expression. Then plot each (x,y)
point on the graph provided.

1.

x	$y = x^2 - 3$
$^-3$	
$^-2.5$	
$^-2$	
$^-1$	
0	
1	
2	
2.5	
3	

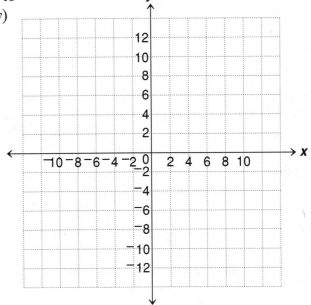

2.

x	$y = ^-2x^2 + 5$
$^-2.5$	
$^-2$	
$^-1.5$	
$^-1$	
0	
1	
1.5	
2	
2.5	

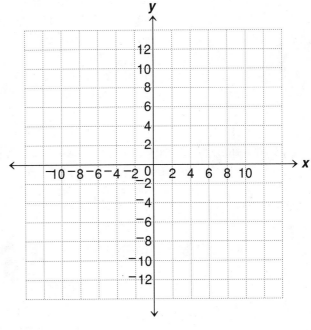

3. If you connect the points in order, what will the

graphs look like? _____

_____

_____

Car Money

Read the paragraph below and answer the questions. Where there is not enough information to answer the question, write **need more data**.

Christine has $380 in her savings account and is making $95 a week working part-time. She would like to buy a used car. She found one for $2,750 that needs new tires and could use new paint. The dealer will replace the tires for $68.53 each. Her father reminded her that sales tax will add $165 to the cost of the car, and that a license fee will add another $155 to the cost. Christine plans to take out a loan for the car and pay $550 as a down payment. The monthly payments, including interest on the loan, will be $135.21. The insurance policy will add $54.87 a month.

1. What will the 4 new tires cost?

   _____

2. What is the purchase price of the car with 4 new tires and new paint?

   _____

3. How much does Christine earn in 52 weeks, or 1 year? _____

4. What is the total cost of the sales tax and license fee? _____

5. How much more does Christine need in order to make the down payment from her savings? _____

6. What is the total cost of the car including new tires, sales tax, and license?

   _____

7. How much is she paying in interest on the car loan? _____

8. What will be Christine's total monthly payment including the loan payment and the insurance? _____

9. To take the car home Christine must pay the down payment plus the sales tax, license fee, and thefirst monthly payment.

   How much is due? _____

10. Christine can save $13.85 a month by getting the loan on her car at her credit union rather than at her bank. How much would them payment be if the loan were from her bank? _____

Fraction Designs

Write the lowest terms fraction for the part shaded.

1.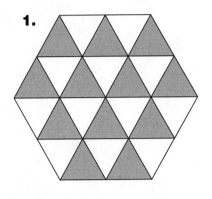

_____

2.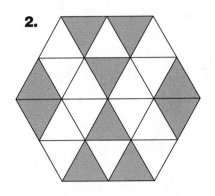

_____

3.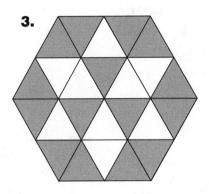

_____

4.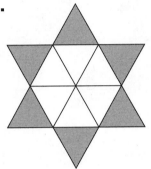

_____

5.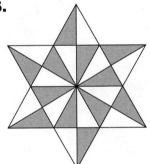

_____

6.

_____

Shade each figure to make a design.

7.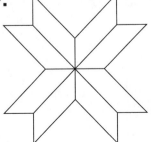

Shade $\frac{1}{4}$.

8.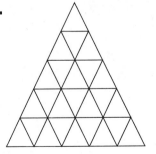

Shade $\frac{3}{5}$.

9.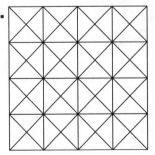

Shade $\frac{3}{8}$.

Name _____

What's The Point?

Change each improper fraction into a mixed number.
Write your answer, then place and label the point on
the number lines below.

1. $\frac{11}{3}$ = _____

2. $\frac{11}{5}$ = _____

3. $\frac{-5}{2}$ = _____

4. $\frac{11}{4}$ = _____

5. $\frac{19}{6}$ = _____

6. $-\frac{11}{2}$ = _____

7. $\frac{27}{5}$ = _____

8. $\frac{22}{3}$ = _____

9. $-\frac{31}{4}$ = _____

10. $\frac{13}{8}$ = _____

11. $\frac{9}{4}$ = _____

12. $-\frac{16}{3}$ = _____

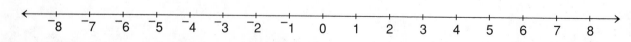

13. $\frac{43}{8}$ = _____

14. $\frac{30}{5}$ = _____

15. $\frac{-7}{1}$ = _____

16. $\frac{14}{3}$ = _____

17. $\frac{24}{6}$ = _____

18. $-\frac{9}{2}$ = _____

19. $\frac{30}{8}$ = _____

20. $\frac{10}{4}$ = _____

21. $-\frac{24}{5}$ = _____

22. $\frac{8}{8}$ = _____

23. $\frac{7}{3}$ = _____

24. $\frac{-21}{4}$ = _____

Comparing Fractions

Without calculating, can you compare $\frac{4}{9}$ to $\frac{1}{2}$?

Half of 9 is $4\frac{1}{2}$. The numerator, 4, is less than $4\frac{1}{2}$. We can easily know, therefore, that $\frac{4}{9} < \frac{1}{2}$.

Use mental math to compare the following fractions to $\frac{1}{2}$. Write <, >, or = in each $\bigcirc$.

1. $\frac{6}{10} \bigcirc \frac{1}{2}$

2. $\frac{3}{7} \bigcirc \frac{1}{2}$

3. $\frac{28}{50} \bigcirc \frac{1}{2}$

4. $\frac{21}{43} \bigcirc \frac{1}{2}$

5. $\frac{3}{6} \bigcirc \frac{1}{2}$

6. $\frac{9}{17} \bigcirc \frac{1}{2}$

7. $\frac{42}{84} \bigcirc \frac{1}{2}$

8. $\frac{40}{79} \bigcirc \frac{1}{2}$

9. $\frac{1111}{2222} \bigcirc \frac{1}{2}$

When rounding to the nearest whole number, round up or down, depending on whether the fractional part is greater or less than $\frac{1}{2}$. Consider these situations.

10. Stuart is 5 ft $5\frac{3}{5}$ in. tall. What height will be printed on his new driver's license if his height is given to the nearest inch?

_____ ft _____ in.

11. Nine students dividing $95 find that they will get $10\frac{5}{9}$ each. Is each getting closer to $10 or $11? _____

Name _____

Calculator Changes

Use the calculator directions and write the decimal display
for each fraction.

	Display		Display		Display
1. $\frac{3}{8}$	_____	**2.** $\frac{7}{11}$	_____	**3.** $\frac{3}{20}$	_____

$3\ \boxed{\div}\ 8\ \boxed{=}$ 　　　 $7\ \boxed{\div}\ 11\ \boxed{=}$ 　　　 $3\ \boxed{\div}\ 20\ \boxed{=}$

Use your calculator to find the missing numerator or
denominator.

4. $\frac{n}{8}$　Display 0.875　　　**5.** $\frac{n}{9}$　Display 0.5555555　　　**6.** $\frac{n}{7}$　Display 0.8571428

$n =$ _____　　　　$n =$ _____　　　　$n =$ _____

7. $\frac{n}{11}$　Display 0.3636363　　　**8.** $\frac{5}{n}$　Display 0.3846153　　　**9.** $\frac{5}{n}$　Display 0.8333333

$n =$ _____　　　　$n =$ _____　　　　$n =$ _____

10. $\frac{5}{n}$　Display 0.5555555　　　**11.** $\frac{5}{n}$　Display 1.6666666　　　**12.** $\frac{5}{n}$　Display 0.4545454

$n =$ _____　　　　$n =$ _____　　　　$n =$ _____

13. $\frac{19}{n}$　Display 0.8636363　　　**14.** $\frac{11}{n}$　Display 0.6111111　　　**15.** $\frac{n}{23}$　Display 0.6956521

$n =$ _____　　　　$n =$ _____　　　　$n =$ _____

Name _____

Fraction Choice

You can add $\frac{3}{4}$ and $\frac{5}{6}$ on your calculator by following these steps.

[ON/AC] [UNIT] 3 [/] 4 [+] [UNIT] 5 [/] 6 [=] [F↺D]

or

[ON/AC] 3 [÷] 4 [=] [M⁺] 5 [÷] 6 [=] [M⁺] [=] [Mᴿ]

$\frac{3}{4} + \frac{5}{6} = \underline{\quad 1.5833333 \quad}$

Add. Use the method you prefer.

1. $\frac{3}{7} + \frac{1}{6} = $ _____

2. $\frac{5}{8} + \frac{3}{5} = $ _____

3. $\frac{4}{5} + \frac{5}{12} = $ _____

4. $\frac{1}{2} + \frac{1}{3} = $ _____

5. $\frac{3}{8} + \frac{8}{9} = $ _____

6. $\frac{1}{5} + \frac{4}{7} = $ _____

7. $\frac{2}{3} + \frac{3}{10} = $ _____

8. $\frac{4}{11} + \frac{1}{8} = $ _____

9. $\frac{5}{7} + \frac{11}{12} = $ _____

10. $\frac{7}{8} + \frac{5}{9} = $ _____

Subtract. Adapt your methods.

$\frac{3}{8} - \frac{1}{4} = \underline{\quad 0.125 \quad}$

11. $\frac{4}{5} - \frac{1}{2} = $ _____

12. $\frac{2}{3} - \frac{2}{5} = $ _____

13. $\frac{8}{9} - \frac{3}{10} = $ _____

14. $\frac{7}{6} - \frac{5}{7} = $ _____

15. $\frac{11}{12} - \frac{3}{8} = $ _____

16. $\frac{5}{8} - \frac{3}{7} = $ _____

17. $\frac{7}{8} - \frac{1}{6} = $ _____

18. $\frac{5}{9} - \frac{1}{3} = $ _____

19. $\frac{4}{11} - \frac{1}{8} = $ _____

20. $\frac{1}{3} - \frac{1}{5} = $ _____

Adding and Subtracting Mixed Numbers

Dear Family,
 Our class has been studying the addition and subtraction of fractions and mixed numbers. Below are examples of the math skills we have been studying.

Write each fraction in lowest terms.

1. $\frac{24}{32}$ _____

2. $\frac{12}{18}$ _____

3. $\frac{40}{48}$ _____

4. $\frac{48}{120}$ _____

Write each mixed number as an improper fraction.

5. $1\frac{5}{8}$ _____

6. $6\frac{1}{4}$ _____

7. $8\frac{9}{10}$ _____

8. $9\frac{2}{7}$ _____

Compare the fractions. Write > or < for each $\bigcirc$.

9. $\frac{4}{7} \bigcirc \frac{5}{8}$

10. $\frac{1}{6} \bigcirc \frac{1}{8}$

11. $\frac{5}{7} \bigcirc \frac{4}{5}$

12. $\frac{6}{7} \bigcirc \frac{17}{20}$

Find the sums.

13.
$$\begin{array}{r} \frac{1}{6} \\ + \frac{3}{4} \\ \hline \end{array}$$

14.
$$\begin{array}{r} 7\frac{1}{4} \\ + 3\frac{1}{3} \\ \hline \end{array}$$

15.
$$\begin{array}{r} 36\frac{1}{2} \\ + 75\frac{5}{6} \\ \hline \end{array}$$

16.
$$\begin{array}{r} \frac{1}{5} \\ \frac{1}{2} \\ + \frac{3}{4} \\ \hline \end{array}$$

17.
$$\begin{array}{r} 4\frac{1}{3} \\ 3\frac{1}{6} \\ + 6\frac{1}{4} \\ \hline \end{array}$$

Find the differences.

18.
$$\begin{array}{r} \frac{2}{3} \\ - \frac{1}{2} \\ \hline \end{array}$$

19.
$$\begin{array}{r} \frac{2}{5} \\ - \frac{1}{10} \\ \hline \end{array}$$

20.
$$\begin{array}{r} 7\frac{5}{6} \\ - 2\frac{1}{8} \\ \hline \end{array}$$

21.
$$\begin{array}{r} 9\frac{7}{8} \\ - 3\frac{1}{3} \\ \hline \end{array}$$

22.
$$\begin{array}{r} 30\frac{1}{4} \\ - 14\frac{2}{3} \\ \hline \end{array}$$

Solve.

23. An electrician needed a piece of wire $75\frac{1}{2}$ in. long. He had a piece of wire that was $28\frac{3}{4}$ in. long. How much more wire does he need?

_____

24. A piece of wire runs $7\frac{1}{2}$ ft along one wall, $6\frac{1}{4}$ ft along another wall, and $5\frac{1}{2}$ ft along a third wall. What is the total length of the wire?

_____

Scrambled Numbers

The steps to the following number "tricks" are
scrambled. First, order them correctly. Then prove the
steps are correct by writing equations to match them.

1. Multiply by 5.   _____   _____

   Pick a number.   _____   _____

   Subtract 4.   _____   _____

   Add 24.   _____   _____

   Divide by 5.   _____   _____

   Subtract 4 again.   _____   _____

   The answer should
   be your number.   _____   _____

2. Multiply by 6.   _____   _____

   Add 6.   _____   _____

   Write your age.   _____   _____

   Divide by 3.   _____   _____

   Subtract 12.   _____   _____

   Your answer should
   be 2.   _____   _____

   Divide by your age.   _____   _____

3. Choose any number and formulate your own number "trick." Your
   trick should have at least 5 steps. Then prove that your trick works.

   _____   _____

   _____   _____

   _____   _____

   _____   _____

   _____   _____

Mixed Number Multiplication

Here is another way to multiply two mixed numbers.

$$4\frac{1}{3} \times 3\frac{1}{4}$$

1 Write the mixed numbers on the sides of a grid.

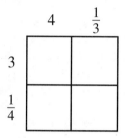

2 Multiply as in a multiplication table.

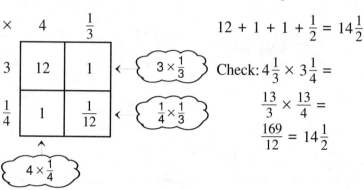

3 Add the numbers inside the grid.

$$12 + 1 + 1 + \frac{1}{2} = 14\frac{1}{2}$$

Check: $4\frac{1}{3} \times 3\frac{1}{4} =$

$$\frac{13}{3} \times \frac{13}{4} =$$

$$\frac{169}{12} = 14\frac{1}{2}$$

Use the grid method to find these products.

1. $4\frac{1}{2} \times 3\frac{3}{4} =$ _____

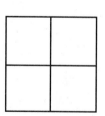

2. $4\frac{1}{2} \times 3\frac{3}{4} =$ _____

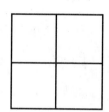

3. $5\frac{2}{3} \times 6\frac{2}{3} =$ _____

4. $8\frac{1}{4} \times 4\frac{5}{8} =$ _____

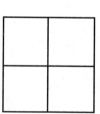

3. $9\frac{3}{4} \times 12\frac{1}{3} =$ _____

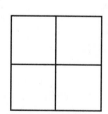

4. $8\frac{3}{12} \times 4\frac{3}{4} =$ _____

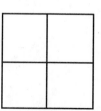

Reciprocals

Give the reciprocal of each number.

1. $\frac{2}{3}$ _____

2. 8 _____

3. $\frac{7}{16}$ _____

4. $\frac{12}{5}$ _____

5. $\frac{13}{18}$ _____

6. 20 _____

7. $\frac{4}{9}$ _____

8. $\frac{7}{4}$ _____

9. $\frac{11}{12}$ _____

10. 62 _____

11. $\frac{1}{50}$ _____

12. $3\frac{1}{2}$ _____

13. $6\frac{2}{3}$ _____

14. $2\frac{7}{9}$ _____

15. $\frac{1}{33}$ _____

16. $\frac{1}{17}$ _____

17. $5\frac{1}{4}$ _____

18. $1\frac{5}{6}$ _____

Give the number for *n* in each equation.

19. $\frac{2}{5} \times n = 1$ _____

20. $3\frac{2}{7} \times n = 1$ _____

21. $\frac{12}{11} \times \frac{11}{12} = n$ _____

22. $n \times \frac{3}{10} = 1$ _____

23. $\frac{5}{9} \times n = 1$ _____

24. $\frac{6}{15} \times n = 1$ _____

25. $n \times \frac{7}{3} = 1$ _____

26. $\frac{3}{8} \times \frac{8}{3} = n$ _____

27. $1\frac{4}{5} \times n = 1$ _____

28. $4\frac{3}{4} \times n = 1$ _____

29. $\frac{7}{10} \times \frac{10}{7} = n$ _____

30. $\frac{16}{5} \times \frac{5}{16} = n$ _____

31. $\frac{21}{4} \times n = 1$ _____

32. $\frac{1}{64} \times n = 1$ _____

Can You Calculate?

Use your calculator to multiply fractions.

$$\frac{1}{5} \times \frac{4}{7} = \underline{0.1142857}$$ [ON/AC] [UNIT] 1 [/] 5 [×] [UNIT] 4 [/] 7 [=] [F D]

Multiply.

1. $\frac{4}{5} \times \frac{3}{4} =$ _____

2. $\frac{5}{12} \times \frac{3}{8} =$ _____

3. $\frac{1}{9} \times \frac{2}{3} =$ _____

4. $\frac{7}{8} \times \frac{2}{13} =$ _____

5. $\frac{5}{12} \times \frac{1}{2} =$ _____

6. $\frac{3}{7} \times \frac{1}{6} =$ _____

7. $\frac{3}{5} \times \frac{1}{3} =$ _____

8. $\frac{8}{9} \times \frac{3}{10} =$ _____

9. $\frac{4}{11} \times \frac{1}{5} =$ _____

10. $\frac{5}{18} \times \frac{7}{23} =$ _____

11. $\frac{14}{15} \times \frac{4}{7} =$ _____

12. $\frac{15}{31} \times \frac{6}{23} =$ _____

13. $\frac{5}{8} \times \frac{3}{14} =$ _____

14. $\frac{9}{43} \times \frac{5}{6} =$ _____

Use your calculator to divide fractions.

$$\frac{7}{8} \div \frac{1}{2} \longrightarrow \frac{7}{8} \times \frac{2}{1} = \underline{1.75}$$ [ON/AC] [UNIT] 7 [/] 8 [÷] [UNIT] 1 [/] 2 [=] [F D]

Divide.

15. $\frac{4}{11} \div \frac{1}{5} =$ _____

16. $\frac{7}{8} \div \frac{1}{3} =$ _____

17. $\frac{11}{12} \div \frac{3}{7} =$ _____

18. $\frac{8}{9} \div \frac{5}{7} =$ _____

19. $\frac{4}{5} \div \frac{2}{5} =$ _____

20. $\frac{2}{3} \div \frac{1}{2} =$ _____

21. $\frac{7}{6} \div \frac{3}{10} =$ _____

22. $\frac{5}{8} \div \frac{3}{8} =$ _____

23. $\frac{5}{9} \div \frac{1}{6} =$ _____

24. $\frac{1}{3} \div \frac{1}{8} =$ _____

25. $\frac{11}{13} \div \frac{2}{7} =$ _____

26. $\frac{9}{20} \div \frac{1}{12} =$ _____

27. $\frac{12}{35} \div \frac{1}{10} =$ _____

28. $\frac{19}{52} \div \frac{1}{3} =$ _____

"Phone" Numbers

A problem may seem difficult if there are large numbers involved. Simplifying the problem by substituting smaller numbers can help you understand the problem.

Phone lines are needed to connect the 10 buildings at the right. A separate line must be used to connect each pair of buildings. How many phone lines are needed?

Draw the number of lines needed for each simpler problem. Then look for a pattern and complete the table.

Number of Buildings	Number of Lines
2	1 = 1 line
3	1 + 2 = 3 lines
4	1 + 2 + 3 = 6 lines
5	1 + 2 + 3 + 4 = 10 lines
6	
7	
8	
9	
10	

Note This in Scientific Notation

Write an equation for each exercise. Then give the
answers in scientific notation. Round to the nearest
tenth.

1. A white blood cell with the diameter of
1.2×10^{-2} mm is magnified 1×10^6 times.
What is the magnified diameter?

_____

_____

2. Light travels about 1.61×10^{10} miles per
day. How far does light travel in one
light-year (365 days)?

_____

_____

3. Mars has a diameter of about 6.76×10^3
km. Saturn's diameter is 1.21×10^5 km.
Saturn's diameter is how many times
Mars's diameter?

_____

_____

4. At one time the population of the United
States was about 2.27×10^8. The area is
9.4×10^6 km². What is the population per
square kilometer? (Round to the ones
place.)

_____

_____

5. A model of the earth has a diameter of 6.4
$\times 10^{-2}$ m. The earth's real diameter is 1.28
$\times 10^7$ m. The earth's diameter is how
many times that of the model?

_____

_____

Name _____

It's a Common Phenomenon

Pick any four numbers and write them in a square.

8 4

1 7

Next connect any two numbers without going across the middle. Subtract the smaller number from the larger number and write the answer at the center of the line.

8 4

1 6 7

Do the same with the other pairs of numbers.

Now connect the center numbers and find their differences.

Repeat for the new numbers.

The common answer is **2.**

Repeat the steps above until you reach a common answer for these combinations of numbers.

1. 3   6 **2.** 1   3 **3.** 3   88

 9   12

         9   27 99   57

4. Make up your own combinations of numbers and repeat the steps above until you reach a common answer.

5. Try starting with the same set of numbers but rearranging the order. Do you end up with the same common difference?

_____

Name _____

It's in the Bag

Inside this bag are some pennies, nickels, and dimes. The ratio of nickels to pennies is 3 to 2. The ratio of dimes to pennies is 5 to 3.

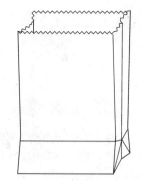

Complete these ratio tables for each of the ratios described above.

1.

nickels	3	6	9	12		
pennies	2	4	6			

dimes	5	10	15	20		
pennies	3	6	9			

2. Is it possible that there are 2 pennies in the bag?

Explain your answer. _____

_____

3. Can there be 3 pennies in the bag? _____

_____

4. What is the smallest number of pennies that would meet the

requirements of both ratios? _____

5. In the completed tables, which other number of pennies

appears to be possible? _____

6. Assume that there are the fewest possible pennies in the

bag. How much money is in the bag? _____

Name _____

Rates and Distances

Jesse and Bart begin walking in opposite directions from the same
point. Jesse walks 3 km each $\frac{1}{2}$ h and Bart walks 2.5 km each $\frac{1}{2}$ h.
Complete this table and use it to solve problems 1 and 2.

	Time	$\frac{1}{2}$ h	1 h	$1\frac{1}{2}$ h	2 h	$2\frac{1}{2}$ h	3 h	6 h	8 h
Distance walked (kilometers)	Jesse	3	6						
	Bart	2.5		7.5					
	Distance apart (km)	5.5							

1. How far apart are Jesse and Bart

after 1 h? _____

after 2 h? _____

after $2\frac{1}{2}$ h? _____

after 8 h? _____

2. In how many hours are Jesse and Bart

11 km apart? _____

33 km apart? _____

16.5 km apart? _____

66 km apart? _____

Two dune buggies leave the same point at the same time heading
in opposite directions. The red one travels 16 km/h and the bronze
one travels 10 km/h. Complete this table and solve the problems.

	Time	1 h	2 h	3 h	4 h	5 h	6 h	8 h
Distance traveled (kilometers)	Red dune buggy							
	Bronze dune buggy							
	Distance apart (km)							

3. How far apart are the dune buggies

after 1 h? _____

after 3 h? _____

after 5 h? _____

after 8 h? _____

4. In how many hours will the dune buggies

be 52 km apart? _____

26 km apart? _____

78 km apart? _____

156 km apart? _____

Name _____

Best Buy

To find the better buy you can compare the unit price of each item.

Example: $\frac{\$2.16}{12}$ = $0.18 per ounce

$\frac{\$3.30}{20}$ = $0.165 per ounce

The 20 oz jar costs less per ounce

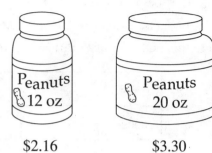

$2.16 $3.30

Use a calculator to find the unit price. Round to the nearest cent. Then ring the better or best buy.

1.

 Polish ✳ 7 oz   Polish ✳ 12 oz

$1.65 $2.13

_____   _____

2.

 Cereal 18 oz   Cereal 20 oz   Cereal 16 oz

$1.52 $1.79 $1.48

_____   _____   _____

3.

 Spray Wax 9 oz   Spray Wax 11 oz    Spray Wax 12 oz

$2.25 $2.68 $2.73

_____   _____   _____

4.

 ☆ Dishwasher Soap ☆ 65 oz   ☆ Dishwasher Soap ☆ 35 oz   ☆ Dishwasher Soap ☆ 32 oz

$3.43 $1.95 $1.85

_____   _____   _____

5.

 FISH STICKS 12 oz $2.18   FISH STICKS 16 oz $2.99

_____

 FISH STICKS 32 oz $5.89   FISH STICKS 30 oz $4.95

_____   _____

6.

 Peanut Butter 28 oz   Peanut Butter 48 oz   Peanut Butter 36 oz

$1.97 $3.26 $2.31

_____   _____   _____

7.

 Apple Juice 46 oz $1.44   Apple Juice 32 oz $1.18

_____   _____

8.

 Toothpaste 6.4 oz $1.65   Toothpaste 7 oz $1.80

_____   _____

 Toothpaste 8.2 oz $2.05   Toothpaste 8.6 oz $2.23

_____   _____

Name _____

Water, Water, Everywhere

An eighth-grade class gathered data on the use of
water at home and wrote some problems that could be
solved using proportions.

Write and solve a proportion for each problem. Use a
calculator if you wish, as in Problems 1 and 2. Round
your answers to the nearest hundredth.

1. Rita's problem: My faucet dripped 25 mL
in 40 s. How much water did it leak
in 1 min?

$$\frac{25}{40} = \frac{n}{60}$$ $n =$ _____

Calculator: 25 $\boxed{\times}$ 60 $\boxed{\div}$ 40 $\boxed{=}$

2. Jackson's problem: When I washed the
dishes I let the hot water run to rinse the
dishes. I measured the rate and got 21 L in
4 min. I figured that I used about 79 L of
hot water in doing the dishes. How long
did I let the water run?

$$\frac{21}{4} = \frac{79}{n}$$ $n =$ _____

Calculator: 4 $\boxed{\times}$ 79 $\boxed{\div}$ 21 $\boxed{=}$

3. Earl's problem: When I took a shower I
found that I used 17 L in 1 min. It takes
me about 8 min to shower. How much
water did I use?

$n =$ _____

4. Kathy's problem: When our faucet was
wide open we filled a 10–L container in
0.7 min. How much water would flow
from that faucet in 1 h?

$n =$ _____

5. Sean's problem: Our bathtub holds 200 L
of water. How long does it take to fill the
tub at a rate of 16 L in 1.5 min?

$n =$ _____

6. Wanda's problem: We used a sprinkler to
water our lawn. We ran the water at a rate
of 42 L per 3 min for 2 h. How much
water did we sprinkle on the lawn?

$n =$ _____

Write and solve two proportion problems about water.

7. _____

_____

_____

_____

_____ = _____ $n =$ _____

8. _____

_____

_____

_____

_____ = _____ $n =$ _____

Name _____

What is the Scale?

Each of the pictures below is drawn to scale. One of the actual dimensions is given. Use a centimeter ruler to measure that dimension and determine the scale.

1.

height

actual width
|← 1 m →|

Scale 1 cm: _____ m
What is the actual
height of the bookshelves? _____

2.

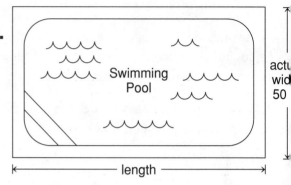

Swimming Pool

actu
wid
50

|← length →|

Scale 1 cm: _____ m
What is the actual
length of the swimming pool? _____

3.

actual height 1.75 m

|← width →|

Scale 1cm:

_____ m

What is the actual width of the window?

4.

Newton   Minden

actual distance
195 km

Glenwood

Scale 1 cm:

_____ m

What is the actual distance from

Minden to Glenwood? _____

From Glenwood to Newton? _____

5.

actual length
|← 1.25 m →|

desk   e
a
          d
    c

b

Scale 1cm:

_____ m

What is the actual length of :

side *a*? _____   side *b*? _____

side *c*? _____   side *d*? _____

side *e*? _____

6.

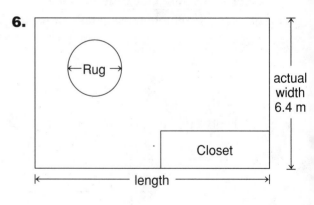

←Rug→

actual width 6.4 m

Closet

|← length →|

Scale 1 cm: _____ m

What is the actual
length of the room? _____

Name _____

Predicting Numbers in a Series

Examine this series of numbers:

1   1   2   3   5   8   13   21   34   55   89   144 . . .

Can you predict the next number in the series?

If not, look at any 2 consecutive numbers. Now look at the next number. What is the relationship between the 3 numbers?

_____

Look at 3 other consecutive numbers. Does the relationship hold?

_____

Do you know the next number in the series? How could you determine any number in the series?

_____

You may know this series. It is named after a 13th-century Italian mathemetician, Leonardo of Pisa, also known as Fibonacci. Surprisingly, this series is found in many places throughout nature. It is related to the Golden Ratio.

Write the ratios of consecutive numbers as decimals.

For example: $\frac{1}{1} = 1, \frac{2}{1} = 2, \frac{3}{2} = 1.5, \frac{5}{3} = 1.66$

Continue the pattern: $\frac{8}{5} =$ _____ , $\frac{13}{8} =$ _____ , $\frac{21}{13} =$ _____

What do you notice about the ratios as the numbers get larger?

Exploring the Triangle

For this activity, you can experiment on a 5 × 5 geoboard
and then record your answer on geoboard paper. If you do
not have a geoboard, you can do the activity right on the paper.

On a geoboard, the smallest distance between 2 pegs is one
unit of length. The smallest square you can make has an
area of one square unit.

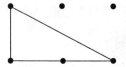

1. What is the area of the triangle shown here? _____

2. Make another triangle with the same area,
   but with a different shape.

3. Make the largest possible geoboard triangles that are
   similar to the ones in Questions 1 and 2. Copy them
   onto geoboard paper.

4. What is the scale for each pair of similar triangles?

   _____

5. What is the ratio of the areas for each pair of
   similar triangles? _____

6. Are the areas of the two larger triangles equal
   to each other? _____

7. What is the largest possible area a triangle on the
   geoboard can have? _____

8. How many different triangles can you make on a
   geoboard that will have that area? _____

Calendar Curiosities I

1. Some dates are special. March 30, 1990, for example, is a "math date" because when written as 3/30/90, the product of the month and the day equals the year. Were there other "math dates" in 1990? If so, what are they?

_____

_____

2. Following 1990, what is the next "math date"?

_____

3. What is the first year folllowing 1990 without a "math date"?

_____

4. Ronald Reagan completed his term as our 40th president in 1989. If George Washington was inaugurated in 1789, what is the average number of years American presidents have served?

_____

5. What is the greatest number of days (Monday–Friday) that you will ever have to attend school during one month?

_____

6. The last year to read the same forward, backward, and upside down was 1881. What will be the next year that this occurs?

_____

May 2001						
SUN	MON	TUE	WED	THU	FRI	SAT
		1	2	3	4	5
6	7	8	9	10	11	12
13	14	15	16	17	18	19
20	21	22	23	24	25	26
27	28	29	30			

On a Tangent

For each triangle, decide whether you would use the tangent ratio to find the variable. If the answer is yes, solve for the variable. If you cannot use the tangent ratio to solve for the variable, write *impossible*.

1.

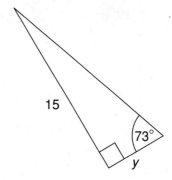

_____

2.

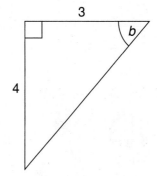

_____

3.

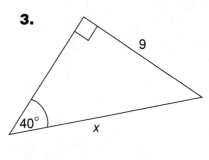

_____

4.

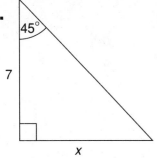

_____

5.

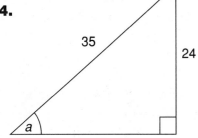

_____

6.

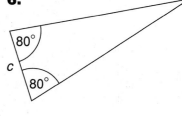

_____

7.

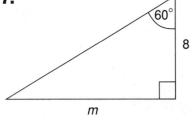

_____

8.

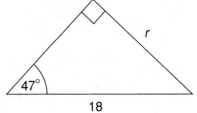

_____

9.

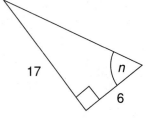

_____

Name _____

Creative Thinking

A group of eighth-grade students were asked to
develop methods for measuring lengths indirectly.
Below are the suggestions they came up with. In each
case: decide whether their reasoning was correct and
explain the reasons for your decision.

1. To measure the height of a flagpole,
students held a 1-foot ruler next to the
pole. Then they measured the length of
each shadow. They knew they could think
of these as similar triangles. Therefore,
they solved for the height of the flagpole
by using the proportion $\frac{1}{h} = \frac{2}{26}$.

Were they correct? _____

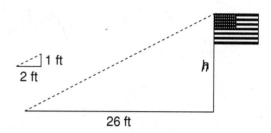

2. To measure the height of a tree, students
measured a distance of 20 meters from the
tree. They placed a large mirror on the
ground and walked another 4 meters from
the tree. A student who was 2 meters tall
when standing on a box could see the top
of the tree when he looked in the mirror.
They used the similar triangles they had
created to set up the proportion $\frac{h}{2} = \frac{20}{4}$.

Were they correct? _____

3. To measure across a pond, a group of
students put a stake at each end. Then
they stretched 2 strings as shown in the
drawing. They staked the other ends of
the strings 6 feet apart. Then they solved
the proportion $\frac{m}{6} = \frac{12}{4}$.

Were they correct? _____

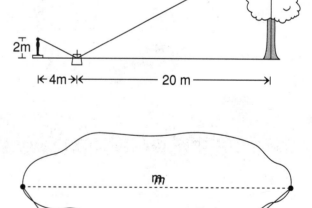

Name _____

A Long Day's Journey

Estimate to order the following trips from shortest (number 1)
to longest (number 10). Then measure each distance with a
centimeter ruler to estimate the actual distance. Write the
measured distance and the correct order.

scale of miles
1 cm: 375 mi

	Estimated Order	Measured Distance	Actual Order
1. Houston to Chicago	_____	_____	_____
2. Seattle to Kansas City	_____	_____	_____
3. Chicago to New York	_____	_____	_____
4. Miami to Seattle	_____	_____	_____
5. Kansas City to Chicago	_____	_____	_____
6. New York to Miami	_____	_____	_____
7. Houston to Seattle	_____	_____	_____
8. Chicago to San Francisco	_____	_____	_____
9. New York to Houston	_____	_____	_____
10. Miami to Kansas City	_____	_____	_____

Name _____

Estimating Percents

Ring the best estimate of the percent of each figure
that is shaded. Write that percent as a decimal.

1.

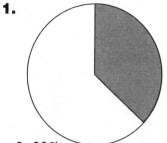

A 23%
B 46%
C 37%
Decimal: _____

2.

A 54%
B 87.5%
C 76.5%
Decimal: _____

3.

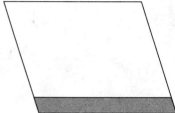

A 14.2%
B 23.4%
C 2.6%
Decimal: _____

4.

A 6.25%
B 11.5%
C 22.3%
Decimal: _____

5.

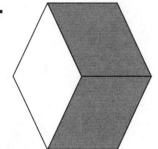

A 55.5%
B 66.7%
C 76.6%
Decimal: _____

6.

A 46.3%
B 52.5%
C 78.2%
Decimal: _____

7.

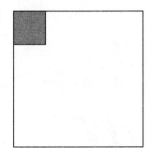

A 16.125%
B 12.5%
C 3.125%
Decimal: _____

8.

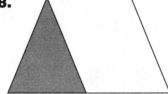

A 33.3%
B 25%
C 15.5%
Decimal: _____

9.

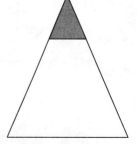

A 20.8%
B 11.1%
C 3.5%
Decimal: _____

Percent Sense

Use what you know about fractions to estimate each percent.

Example:  About what percent of the jar is filled?

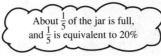

About $\frac{1}{5}$ of the jar is full, and $\frac{1}{5}$ is equivalent to 20%

The jar is about 20% full.

Ring the best estimate.

1. About what percent of the distance has been traveled?

Start   End

A 80%   **B** 60%   **C** 20%

2. About what percent of the jar is filled?

A 66%   **B** 75%   **C** 88%

3. About what percent of the pie is gone?

A 20%   **B** 16%   **C** 10%

4. About what percent of the cake is left?

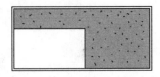

A 60%   **B** 75%   **C** 80%

5. About what percent has been mowed?

A 66%   **B** 75%   **C** 88%

6. About what percent of the desktop is painted dark?

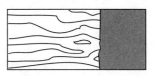

A 25%   **B** 33%   **C** 45%

7. About what percent of the envelope is covered by the stamp?

A 12%   **B** 16%   **C** 20%

8. About what percent of the bulletin board is covered?

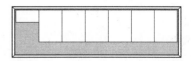

A 50%   **B** 60%   **C** 75%

Name _____

Percent Possibilities

You may have heard a coach say that he likes an athlete because "he gives 110 percent every day."

Is it possible for an athlete, or anyone else, to give 110 percent of

his or her ability? _____ If 100 percent means

all of something, is it really possible for anything to be greater

than 100 percent? _____

Think about each of the following statements. Is the situation possible? Does it make sense?

1. An ice cream cone may be 150 percent full.

_____

2. A one-quart milk container may be 125 percent full.

_____

3. If income tax rates continue to rise, the rate may one day be 110 percent.

_____

4. If sales tax rates continue to rise, the rate may one day be 110 percent.

_____

5. A TV weather forecaster says that there is a 100 percent chance of rain.

_____

_____

6. A teacher tells a parent that her child is working at 150 percent of her ability.

_____

8. At a clearance sale, an item is advertised as 125% off the original price.

_____

7. One student scores 130 percent of another student's grade on an exam.

_____

10. The price of gasoline has increased more that 100 percent in the past ten years.

_____

9. You can have 113 percent of a dollar in coins in your pocket.

_____

Amazing Facts

Did you know that

▶ A hot-air balloon in 1783 rose to a height equal to about 4% of the 72,000 feet achieved by a helium balloon in 1935?

▶ A diver using scuba equipment has reached a depth equal to a little more than 1% of the 35,802 feet reached in a diving machine?

▶ The distance from London to Moscow is 37% of the 4,665-mile distance from New York to Moscow?

▶ The world's highest active volcano, Cotopaxi in Ecuador, is 67% of the height of the world's highest mountain, Mt. Everest, at 29,028 feet?

▶ The world's deepest known cave, Pierre St.-Martin in France and Spain, is about 280% as deep as the height of the world's tallest building, the Sears Tower in Chicago, at 1,559 feet?

▶ The world's longest suspension bridge at Hull, England, is about 110% of the length of the 4,200-foot-long Golden Gate Bridge at San Francisco?

Now complete each statement.

1. In 1783 a hot-air balloon rose about   **A** 300 ft   **B** 3,000 ft   **C** 30,000 ft

2. A scuba diver has reached a depth of   **A** 437 ft   **B** 43.7 ft   **C** 4,370 ft

3. The distance from London to Moscow is   **A** 174 mi   **B** 1,749 mi   **C** 5,027 mi

4. The height of Cotopaxi is   **A** 19,344 ft   **B** 1,934 ft   **C** 193.4 ft

5. The depth of the cave Pierre St.-Martin is   **A** 43,700 ft   **B** 437 ft   **C** 4,370 ft

6. The length of the bridge at Hull, England, is   **A** 426 ft   **B** 4,626 ft   **C** 46,626 ft

Traveling Time

You can use your calculator to solve percent problems.

Example:

The flight to the moon in *Apollo II* took about 3 days. It took Christopher Columbus and his crew about 63 days to sail across the Atlantic Ocean.

What percent of 63 is 3?

Try one of these on your calculator to solve the problem.

$$3 \; [\div] \; 63 \; [\%] \; [=]$$
or $$3 \; [\div] \; 63 \; [\times] \; 100 \; [=]$$

Apollo II's flight time was about 4.8% of Columbus's sailing time.

Follow the instructions for Problems 1 and 2.

1. What percent of 75 is 30? _____

$$30 \; [\div] \; 75 \; [\%] \; [=]$$
or $$30 \; [\div] \; 75 \; [\times] \; 100 \; [=]$$

2. What percent of 25 is 8? _____

$$8 \; [\div] \; 25 \; [\%] \; [=]$$
or $$8 \; [\div] \; 25 \; [\times] \; 100 \; [=]$$

Solve. Round your answers to the nearest tenth.

3. What percent of 48 is 60? _____

4. What percent of 65 is 53.3? _____

5. What percent of 140 is 35? _____

6. What percent of 120 is 39? _____

7. What percent of 72 is 9? _____

8. What percent of 70 is 56? _____

9. What percent of 54 is 40.5? _____

10. What percent of 3,200 is 864? _____

11. What percent of 354 is 59? _____

12. What percent of 280 is 175? _____

13. What percent of 205 is 246? _____

14. What percent of 12 is 65? _____

15. In 1849 it took about 166 days to cross the United States by covered wagon. The same trip by stage coach in 1860 took 60 days. What percent of 166 is 60?

_____

16. In the 1870s it took about 264 hours to cross the United States by train. In 1923 it took about 26 hours to fly coast-to-coast. What percent of 264 is 26?

_____

17. In 1938 it took 17.5 hours to fly across the United States. In 1975 the flight took 5 hours. What percent of 17.5 is 5?

_____

18. A 747 jet flies coast-to-coast in 300 minutes. The space shuttle Columbia crosses the United States in only 8 minutes. What percent of 300 is 8?

_____

Name _____

Cost + Tax – Rebate

Examine each set of data. Then find the total amount paid and ring it. Rebates always come after taxes and are on the total amount paid, including tax. Round to the nearest penny when necessary.

Total Amount Paid

1. Cost of item: $50
Taxes: state 4%   city 3%
Rebate: none

A $53.50   **B** $53.56

C $57.00

2. Cost of items: $24, $30
Taxes: state 5%   city 2%
Rebate: $10

A $45.80   **B** $47.08

C $47.78

3. Cost of items: $9, $7.50, $3
Taxes: state 3%   city 1%
Rebate: $1.50

A $18.72   **B** $18.78

C $18.79

4. Cost of items: $29.90, $37.50
Taxes: state 4%   city 5%
Rebate: 10%

A $66.23   **B** $66.24

C $66.12

5. Cost of items: $75, $109.99
Taxes: state 6%   city 2%
Rebates: $10 on $75, 15% on $109.99

A $174.79   **B** $171.97

C $149.84

6. Cost of items: $37.10, $12.05
Taxes: state 3%   city 5%
Rebates: 5% on $37.10, 10% on $12.05

A $50.01   **B** $49.77

C $49.10

In Reverse

What number belongs in the first box? Work backward to find out.
Start with the last box and perform the inverse of each operation.

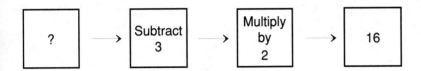

Do you see why 11 belongs in the first box? Explain your thinking.

_____

Complete these using the same strategy.

1. [?] → [Subtract 3] → [Divide by 2] → [Add 5] → [25] _____

2. [?] → [Divide by 5] → [Add 7] → [Subtract 17] → [0] _____

3. [?] → [Subtract 7] → [Divide by 2] → [Add $\frac{1}{2}$] → [$1\frac{1}{2}$] _____

Now fill in the frames to create a correct sequence.

4. [?] → [Subtract] → [Divide by] → [10] _____

5. [?] → [Subtract] → [Divide by] → [Add] → [36] _____

Create your own sequence. Ask a classmate to solve it.

6. [ ] → [ ] → [ ] → [ ] → [ ]

Percent Clues

Decide which test each student took.

Quiz 25 questions	**Final** 50 questions

Which test?

1. Jan missed 2 questions and scored 92%. _____

2. Mary missed 5 questions and scored 90%. _____

3. Andrew got 20 questions correct and scored 80%. _____

4. Roberto missed 4 questions and scored 84%. _____

Below are the records of games won and lost by four teams.
Decide which team is described in each problem.

Eagles		Bulldogs		Lions		Giants	
Won	Lost	Won	Lost	Won	Lost	Won	Lost
7	8	5	10	9	6	12	3

Which team?

5. This team won 33% of its games. _____

6. This team won 80% of its games. _____

7. This team lost 67% of its games. _____

8. This team won 60% of its games. _____

Calculators Can Be Wrong!

Calculators are programmed to work in one of two ways:

► Left-to-right, ignoring the order of operations, or
► Algebraically, following the order of operations.

Examine these sequences to see the difference.

Left-to-right	Algebraic
yields 32	yields 26

Which is correct? _____

Most of the time—but not always—an algebraically
programmed calculator will evaluate an expression correctly.

Examine this expression. Think about the sequence of
keys you would press to evaluate it.

Left-to-right	Algebraic
yields 3	yields 17.4

Which is correct? _____

Explain why the other answer is incorrect. _____

_____

Now decide whether each of these expressions was
evaluated using a left-to-right or an algebraic calculator
and whether the result is correct. If you think both types
of calculator would give the same result, indicate that.

1. $7 - 4 \times 3 = {}^- 5$ _____

2. $\frac{8}{4} + 3 = 5$ _____

3. $6 + \frac{10}{5} + 3 = 6.2$ _____

4. $\frac{45 + 15}{20} = 45.75$ _____

5. $7 + 4 - \frac{1}{2} = 10.5$ _____

To Lease or Not to Lease

Have you thought about owning your own car? Today, many people no longer buy cars; instead they prefer to lease them. Many leases on new cars run for 5 years.

Assume that you are about to lease a new car. You will need some questions answered, such as the ones below. You can probably find some of the information in the automobile ads in your local newspaper. For the rest, ask an adult in your home or visit an automobile dealership. As you answer each question, ask yourself whether your answer is reasonable.

1. What kind of car would you like to lease? _____

2. What would the car cost if you were to buy it new? _____

3. On a 5-year lease, how much is the down payment? _____
The monthly payment? _____
What is the total of the payments for 5 years? _____

4. How many miles are you allowed to drive during the 5 years without having to pay an extra mileage charge? _____

5. How much is the charge per mile for miles driven beyond the answer to Question 4? _____

6. Suppose during the 5 years you drove a total of 98,500 miles. How much would you owe just for the extra mileage charges? _____

7. How does the total of lease and mileage charges compare with the cost of buying the car new? _____

8. How much will it cost you to insure your car per month? _____
For 5 years? _____

9. What is the average cost of a gallon of gasoline where you live? _____

10. How many miles will your car travel on one gallon of gasoline? _____

11. If you did drive 98,500 miles during the 5 years, how much would you spend just on gasoline? _____

12. Assuming your car needs no repairs, how much will you have spent after 5 years on payments, insurance, mileage, and gasoline? _____

Keeping up with the Jones

Jones Company
$9.50 per hour
1.5 times $9.50 for hours over 20
6.2% for sales up to $5,000
12.5% for sales over $5,000

Smith Company
$10.50 per hour
1.5 times $10.50 for hours over 25
4.8% for sales up to $2,500
10.2% for sales over $2,500

1. Mary McCarthy

Office hours	15
Sales	$2,000

Jones Co. _____

Smith Co. _____

2. Daniel Dunsay

Office hours	20
Sales	$2,500

Jones Co. _____

Smith Co. _____

3. Rosemary Reid

Office hours	18
Sales	$5,400

Jones Co. _____

Smith Co. _____

4. Henry Herr

Office hours	30
Sales	$1,500

Jones Co. _____

Smith Co. _____

5. Valerie VanMiert

Office hours	35
Sales	$2,400

Jones Co. _____

Smith Co. _____

6. Kevin Kelly

Office hours	37
Sales	$4,000

Jones Co. _____

Smith Co. _____

7. When is it better to work for the Jones Co.?

_____

8. When is it better to work for the Smith Co.?

_____

Name _____

Comparison Shopping

Sam's: Save $\frac{1}{4}$ of regular price

Al's: On sale for $350

Dan's: Save 20% of regular price

Regular price $495

1. Which store has the best buy?   _____

2. How much could you save at this store?   _____

Sam's: Save $\frac{1}{5}$ of regular price

Al's: On sale for $129

Dan's: Save 15% of regular price

Regular price $150

3. Which store has the best buy?   _____

4. How much could you save at this store?   _____

Sam's: Save 35%

Al's: On sale for $495

Dan's: On sale for $\frac{1}{3}$ off

Regular price $750

5. Which store has the best buy?   _____

6. How much could you save at this store?   _____

7. Which is the better deal on a $200 bike? `_____

   A: a discount of 15% followed by a discount of 25%

   B: a discount of 25% followed by a discount of 15%

Name _____

Estimating Percents

Estimate the part of each figure that is not shaded.
Write it as a fraction, then as a percent.

1.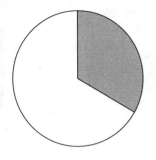

_____ = _____

2.

_____ = _____

3.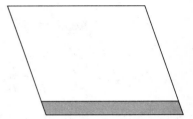

_____ = _____

4.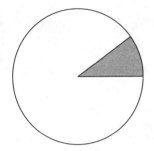

_____ = _____

5.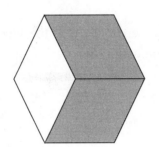

_____ = _____

6.

_____ = _____

7.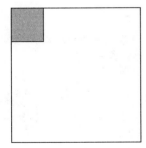

_____ = _____

8.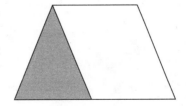

_____ = _____

9.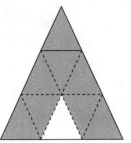

_____ = _____

Advertising Techniques

Dear Family,

   Your eighth grader has been studying the claims that are made by advertisers. Read advertisements in newspapers or magazines with her or him. Cut out the advertisements and classify them according to the type of propaganda technique they use to sell their product. The following are some types of propaganda techniques you may find:

► Jump on the bandwagon

► Appeal to authority or testimony

► Act fast before it's too late

► Something for nothing

► Transferring the feeling

Paste some examples of advertisements in the space below. Write the propaganda technique that is used. You may find some other techniques.

Variations on a Problem

Sometimes a word problem is a variation of a problem you already know how to solve. To vary the problem, the writer has

    A changed the context/setting
    B changed the numbers
    C changed the number of conditions
    D reversed the given and the wanted information
    E a combination of the above

Look at the word problem below. Then look at the variation of the word problem and decide what principle above was used to vary the original problem.

> At a meeting, every person shook hands with each other person exactly one time. There were 12 people at the meeting. How many handshakes were there?

1. 12 students were at a Ping-Pong tournament. Each student played one game against each other student. How many games were played? _____

2. At a meeting, every person shook hands with each other person exactly one time. If there were 66 handshakes, how many people were at the meeting? _____

3. At a meeting, every person but the chairperson shook hands with each person exactly one time. The chairperson shook hands with everyone twice. There were 12 people at the meeting. How many handshakes were there? _____

4. At a meeting, every person shook hands with each other person exactly one time. There were 20 people at the meeting. How many handshakes were there?

_____

5. 20 students were at a Ping-Pong tournament. Each student played one game against each other student. How many games were played? _____

6. How can recognizing that one problem is a variation of another help you solve it?

_____

_____

_____

_____

Name _____

Discounts on Discounts

A department store discounts everything in the store
10%. Bicycle helmets are on sale with an additional
10% off the already discounted price. Kris and Glen
each computed the sale price of the helmet
after two discounts.

Regular price:	$96.00
First discount rate:	10%
Second discount rate:	10%

Kris' Work

10% + 10% = 20% off

$96.00
× 0.20
_____
$19.20 ⟵ Total
discount

$96.00
− 19.20
_____
$76.80 ⟵ Sale
price

Glen's Work

$96.00
× 0.20
_____
$ 9.60 ⟵ First
discount

$86.40
× 0.10
_____
$ 8.64 ⟵ Second
discount

$96.00
− 9.60
_____
$86.40 ⟵ First
sale
price

$86.40
− 8.64
_____
$77.76 ⟵ Second
sale
price

1. Whose work is correct? _____

Use the correct method to find each sale price. Complete the table.
Round discounts to the nearest cent.

	Regular price	First discount rate	Second discount rate	Sale price
2.	$56.00	5%	10%	
3.	$38.40	20%	20%	
4.	$106.30	5%	15%	
5.	$25.75	30%	10%	
6.	$2,050.00	10%	20%	
7.	$4,038.00	5%	25%	

Calculating Percent

Dear Family,
    Our class is studying applications of percent. Below are examples of the math skills we are studying.

Write each percent as a decimal.

1. 53% _____   **2.** 6.3% _____   **3.** 70% _____   **4.** 145% _____

Write the lowest-terms fraction for each percent.

5. 95% _____   **6.** 4.25% _____   **7.** 1.25% _____   **8.** 0.05% _____

Find the percent of each number.

9. 2% of 150 _____   **10.** 14% of 350 _____   **11.** 3.5% of 600 _____

Find the interest and the amount. Use $I = PRT$ and $A = P + I$.

12. $P = \$2,500$

   $R = 15\%$ per year $I =$ _____

   $T = 2$ years $A =$ _____

13. $P = \$900$

   $R = 9\%$ per year $I =$ _____

   $T = 6$ months $A =$ _____

14. What percent of 30 is 21? _____

15. What percent of 325 is 65? _____

16. 56% of what number is 28? _____

17. 30% of what number is 4.5? _____

Solve.

18. In an election for class secretary, Eric won 84% of the votes. If 352 students voted, about how many voted for Eric? _____

19. Layla borrowed $650 for 2 years. The interest rate was 12% per year. What amount did she have to repay? _____

Football Scores

These charts show football scores for games played by
the Hawks and for games played by the Wildcats.

Hawks	17	14	21	17	7	3	28	10	20	14
Opponent	3	14	13	21	3	13	7	14	7	35

Wildcats	21	13	7	13	7	17	30	20
Opponent	17	3	7	10	28	13	14	21

1. Complete this chart using the data above.

Team	Games won	Games lost	Games tied	Games played
Hawks				
Wildcats				

2. Make circle graphs to show the number of games won,
lost, and tied for each team.

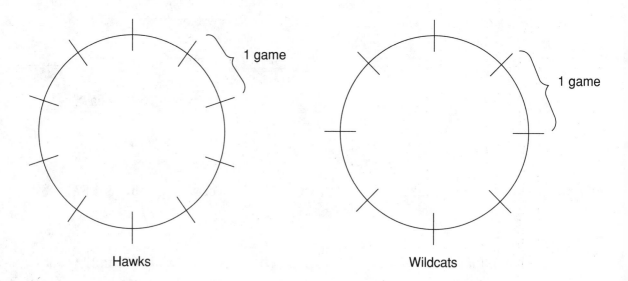

Hawks   1 game

Wildcats   1 game

3. Even though each team won 5 games, one team had a

better record. Which team? _____

Name _____

Strategic Planning

Identify the problem solving strategy needed to solve
each problem. Then write a problem that uses the same
strategy and give it to a friend to solve.

1. Aaron is older than Joseph and has a cat. David is not
as old as Joseph and has a dog. Bob is 3 days older
than Joseph and has a cat and a dog. Aaron is the
oldest. List the boys from oldest to the youngest.
Which boy owns a fish?

_____

2. _____

_____

_____

_____

3. 599 teams will play a single elimination baseball
tournament—one loss and you are out. How many
games must be played to determine a champion?

_____

4. _____

_____

_____

5. The sum of five consecutive numbers is 155. Find the
numbers.

_____

6. _____

_____

How Many Choices?

Norma is having a difficult time choosing a sweater for her sister's birthday gift. Below are the choices listed in a mail-order catalog.

Color: blue, purple, red
Style: buttons, no buttons
Fabric: wool, nylon, cotton

1. Fill in the tree diagram to show all of the possible choices.

2. How many possible combinations are there?

_____

3. How many of the possible sweater choices are

purple?   _____

nylon with buttons?   _____

blue without buttons?   _____

blue wool with buttons?   _____

red cotton?   _____

orange?   _____

4. Write one of the following phrases in the blank to make the sentence true.

are red   are cotton

have buttons   are wool

Half of the possible choices _____

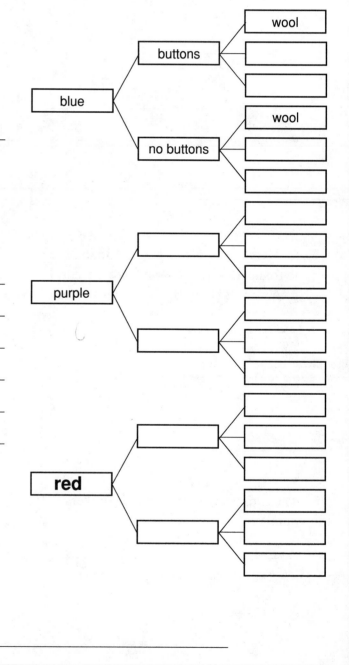

Name _____

Permutations for Part of a Group

If 8 students are to be put in order, the number of
permutations is: $8! = 8 \times 7 \times 6 \times 5 \times 4 \times 3 \times 2 \times 1$.

If only 3 of the 8 are to be put in order, the
permutations are $8 \times 7 \times 6$. Use only the 3 greatest
factors. Do not use the $5 \times 4 \times 3 \times 2 \times 1 = 5!$ from the
original selection.

To find the number of ways 3 items from 8 can be put
in order, do the following:

$$\frac{8!}{(8-3)!} = \frac{8!}{5!} = \frac{8 \times 7 \times 6 \times 5 \times 4 \times 3 \times 2 \times 1}{5 \times 4 \times 3 \times 2 \times 1} = 8 \times 7 \times 6 = 3,136$$

The formula for putting x items from n in order is:

$\frac{n!}{(n-x)!}$ (Remember to cancel like factors from the numerator and denominator.)

Find the number of permutations for the following.

1. Put 4 items from 6 in order. _____

2. Put 1 item from 8 in order. _____

3. Put 5 items from 20 in order. _____

4. Put 8 items from 8 in order. _____

5. A family has 3 children. They had a boy, then a girl, then another girl. (b, g, g). List all of the
other possible outcomes for a family of 3 children.

_____

_____

Name _____

Boxed In

A carton manufacturing company was seeking an
efficient way to create a box in the shape of an open
cube. One of their designers suggested they could use
any of the 12 pentomino shapes. All they needed was
to determine the one that was least expensive to
manufacture.

A pentomino is like a domino, except that it consists of
5 squares. Each side must share a **complete** side with
at least one other square.

These are 2 of the 12 possible   These are not pentominoes:
pentominoes:

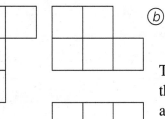

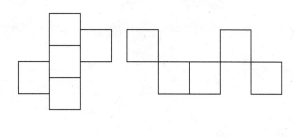

These 2 are
the same; they
are congruent.

Use a sheet of centimeter graph paper. Copy the 2
different pentominoes shown here. Then draw the
other 10 pentominoes. Remember, if 2 shapes are
congruent, they are not different pentominoes.

Now examine the 12 shapes. Was the designer correct?
Can all 12 pentominoes be folded along borders to
form an open cube? If you are not sure, trace and cut
out the entire pentomino and experiment. However,
once you have cut around the perimeter, do not make
any other cuts.

Which ones can be folded into open cubes? _____

Permutations

An arrangement of a group of objects in a certain order is called a permutation.
There are 6 possible permutations for the colors red, yellow, and blue.

red, yellow, blue	red, blue, yellow
yellow, red, blue	yellow, blue, red
blue, yellow, red	blue, red, yellow

Give the number of possible permutations for each of the following groups. Show how you determined your answer.

1. six people standing in a row

_____

2. the letters in the word *today*

_____

3. a vase of each of these flowers: roses, daisies, mums

_____

4. these names on a class list: Eleanor, Daryl, Katelyn, Bobby, Dot, Barbara, Len

_____

5. the first four finishers in a race

_____

6. a row of each of these vegetables in a garden: beans, peas, carrots, lettuce, squash, turnips, radishes, onions

_____

7. What conclusion can you draw about finding the number of possible permutations for a number of objects?

_____

_____

_____

The Combination Formula

If 3 items are to be selected from 7, the number of combinations is:

$$\frac{\text{permutations 3 from 7}}{\text{permutations 3 from 3}} = \frac{7 \times 6 \times 5}{3 \times 2 \times 1}$$

This is the same as $\dfrac{7 \times 6 \times 5 \times 4 \times 3 \times 2 \times 1}{3 \times 2 \times 1 \times 4 \times 3 \times 2 \times 1} = \dfrac{7!}{3!\,(7-3)!}$

The formula for choosing 3 items from 7 is: $= \dfrac{7!}{3!\,(7-3)!}$

The formula for choosing x items from n is: $= \dfrac{n!}{x!\,(n-x)!}$

(Remember to cancel factors from the numerator and denominator.)

Find the number of combinations.

1. Choose 4 items from 6. _____

2. Choose 8 items from 11. _____

3. Choose 1 item from 9. _____

4. Choose 15 items from 17. _____

5. Choose 18 items from 18. _____

6. Choose 6 items from 12. _____

7. A family has 4 children. They had a boy, then another boy, then a girl, then a boy. (b, b, g, b). List all other possible outcomes for a family of 4 children.

_____

_____

_____

_____

_____

_____

Name _____

Pascal's Perplexing Patterns

The patterns in Pascal's triangle have been known for
hundreds of years.

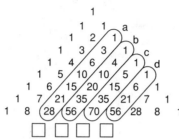

You can use the pattern in each diagonal row to predict
the next number in that row. You can add the two numbers
directly above to verify your prediction.

For example, in diagonal row **a**, you would probably predict
that the next number is 36. This is because the difference
between each pair of numbers is increasing by 1. You could
check your prediction by adding the 8 and 28 directly above.

Foe diagonal rows **b**, **c**, and **d**, do the following:

1. Predict the next number in the row.

_____

2. Check the accuracy of you prediction.

3. Explain the pattern you used to answer question 1.

_____

_____

_____

There are many other patterns in Pascal's triangle. Some
are not easy to see. Can you find a pattern for each horizontal row?

_____

_____

Here is a tough one: Can you find a pattern for prime numbers?

_____

_____

_____

Name _____

Graphing Inequalities

Inequalities can be graphed on a coordinate grid. First
graph the inequality as if it were an equation. Then look
for points on the grid that satisfy the inequality.

For example, to graph the inequality $x + y < 6$, first
draw a graph of $x + y = 6$. Find ordered pairs so that
the x value and the y value add to 6. What points are
already marked on the grid? _____

Complete this table for $x + y = 6$

x	y	$x + y$	Coordinate Point
0	6	6	(0,6)
1	☐	6	☐
2	4	6	☐
☐	3	6	☐
4	☐	6	☐
5	☐	6	☐
6	0	6	☐

Fill in the missing points on the coordinate grid and
connect them. What does the graph of $x + y = 6$ look like? _____

_____

On which side of the graph of $x + y = 6$ would you
expect to find points that satisfy the inequality $x + y < 6$? _____

What are some points that satisfy the inequality $x + y < 6$? _____

_____

On a sheet of centimeter graph paper, label two sets of
x and y axes. Use the model explained here to graph and
find 3 solutions for each of these inequalities:

$$x + y < 10 \qquad x + y > 7$$

Incorrect "Solutions"

Each of the following problems has been solved, or so it seems. The answer given appears to be logical until you look closely. The correct answer is also given. Put yourself in the place of the people who worked on these problems. What reasoning do you think they used to arrive at their solutions? What should they have been thinking?

Write your answers on the lines below each problem.

1. A mouse fell into a 10-m-deep hole. Each day he climbed 3 m up the side, but each night he slid back 2 m. How many days did it take him to get out of the hole?
"Solution": 10 days
Real answer: 8 days

_____

_____

_____

2. The time required for a clock to chime 6 times is 5 seconds. How much time is required for the same clock to chime 12 times?
"Solution": 10 seconds
Real Answer: 11 seconds

_____

_____

_____

3. Each year the NCAA invites 64 teams to compete for the national basketball title. If a team loses a game it is eliminated. How many games are needed to find a champion?
"Solution": 64 games
Real answer: 63 games

_____

_____

_____

4. Roberto spent $20 on a calculator, then sold it for $25. He later bought it back for $30 and finally sold it for $35. How much money did he make in all?
"Solution": $20
Real answer: $10

_____

_____

_____

Name _____

License Plates

A certain state has the following rules for making
license plates.

Rule A: All numbers and letters are chosen by chance and have
an equal chance of occuring. Numbers and letters may
be used only once in a license plate.

Rule B: A license plate may consist of 1 number followed by 4
letters or 2 numbers followed by 3 letters.

Rule C: The letters may not be arranged to form an English word.

Rule D: The numbers may not be arranged to form an odd number.

Given these rules, what is the sample space of possible
license plates for each of the following groups of
letters and numbers.

1. 3, 7, 2, A, C, R

_____

_____

_____

_____

2. 1, 8, 9, T, P, O, S

_____

_____

_____

_____

_____

_____

3. Choose a set of 3 numbers and 4 letters. Write the sample space of all license plates for your
choices following the same rules.

_____

_____

_____

_____

_____

_____

Data Analysis

Name _____

Luck of the Draw

The student council president at Whelms Junior High is drawing
a name out of a hat to select a council member to represent the
student body at a reception for the mayor.

Council Members							
Member	Grade	Member	Grade	Member	Grade	Member	Grade
Dan Jones	8	Jim Monroe	9	Tom Mayer	9	Sue Wiley	9
Mary Mifume	8	Kate Wright	7	Max Doria	9	Judy Stein	8
Joan Carr	7	Jenny Pitt	9	Debbie Lee	7	Mandy Jacobs	7
Miranda Perez	9	Ben Hope	9	Anna Sanchez	8	Russell Young	8
Norm Gant	8	Stew Barns	8	Jack Toth	7	Steve Kasko	9

Complete the frequency chart as needed in order to answer
the questions below. Use the probability formula to compute
your answers.

1. What is the probability of drawing
the name of a council member

Description	Frequency
female	
male	
eighth grader	

who is female? _____

who is male? _____

who is an eighth grader? _____

who is not a seventh grader? _____

who is a ninth grader? _____

who is a male ninth grader? _____

2. What is the probability of drawing the
name of either a male or a female?

_____

3. The probability of drawing the name of
a student who is 14 years old is $\frac{2}{5}$. How
many students are 14 years old?

_____

4. The probability of drawing the name
of a student who has a class with Mr.
Cartwright is $\frac{3}{10}$. How many of Mr.
Cartwright's students are in the drawing?

_____

TS-8   Use with text pages 336–337.   **123**

Name _____

Chances Are

> Dear Family,
>   Our class has just studied probability. Below are examples of the math skills we have been studying.

Give the probability of each outcome for a number cube numbered 1 through 6.

1. What is $P(5)$? _____

2. What is P (even number)? _____

3. What is $P(7)$? _____

4. What is P (odd number)? _____

Study the two spinners and answer the following questions.

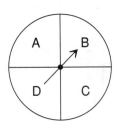 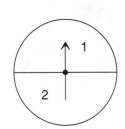

5. How many events are possible when both spinners are spun? _____

6. What is $P(B, 1)$? _____

7. What are the odds in favor of $(D,2)$? _____

8. What are the odds against $(C,2)$? _____

Toss a number cube twice and answer the following questions.

9. Are the events dependent or independent? _____

10. What is $P(5,6)$ _____

Predict the number of times each event will occur.

11. Spin the spinner 120 times.

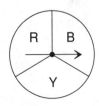

Event: R
$P(R) = \frac{1}{3}$ _____

12. Spin the spinner 125 times.

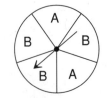

Event: A
$P(A) \frac{2}{5}$ _____

Unequal Branches

The probabilities along different branches of a tree are not always equal.

1. Suppose that the bag to the right contains 5 blue marbles and 3 red marbles. If you choose one, replace it, and choose another, what is the probability that you will have drawn 2 blue marbles?

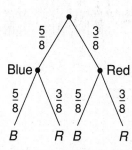

The tree diagram to the right shows the different probabilities associated with this experiment.

What is the probability of a blue followed by another blue? _____

How many possible outcomes are there if you choose two marbles? _____

What is the sum of the probabilities of all the possible outcomes? _____

2. Suppose that after you choose one marble, you examine it but do not replace it in the bag. What is the probability that if you choose a second marble you will have drawn 2 blue marbles? Use the tree diagram to the right to help you.

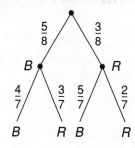

_____

Under these conditions, is any outcome more likely than a blue marble followed

by a blue marble? _____

Which is the least

likely outcome? _____

Strategies

Solve each problem.

1. In designing a flag for itself, a newly emerging nation attempted to place stars on the flag in rows of 3, but found 1 more star was needed. It had the same result when it tried to arrange the stars in rows of 4. When it placed the stars in rows of 5, however, there were none left over. If there were fewer than 100 stars on the flag, how many stars might there have been? Explain.

_____

_____

_____

_____

_____

2. A well-known problem asks, "If you have 5 red socks and 5 green socks in your drawer and reach in without looking, what is the fewest number of socks you must take out to be certain of having a pair of the same color?" When you have solved that problem, consider this: If, in another galaxy, the same problem were faced by a being requiring a trio, rather than a pair of matching socks, what is the fewest number of socks she/he/it would have to take out to be certain of having 3 of the same color?

_____

4. A bag of marbles can be divided equally among either 2, 3, 4, 5, or 6 friends. What is the smallest number of marbles that can be in the bag? Can there be any other number of marbles less than 100 in the bag?

3. An unusual bottle-making factory determines the number of bottles to be made each day by randomly arranging the digits 1, 2, 3, 4, and 5 to form a 5-digit number. However, they will make only a number of bottles that can be packaged in cartons of 3 with none left over. How many days in a row can the factory go before it must repeat a number of bottles?

_____

Shared Birthdays

Were you surprised to find that only 23 people were needed to give a 0.51 chance of having a shared birthday?

You can do the arithmetic to see why this is so. It is not difficult if you use a calculator. The easiest way is to find the probability of having *no shared birthday* and then to subtract that probability from 1. This works because the two possibilities—*no shared birthday* and *shared birthdays*—add to exactly 1.

Using a leap year with 366 days, consider the following:

► With only one person, whose birthday can be on any of the 366 days, there is a 366/366 = 1 chance or certainty of no shared birthday.

► With 2 people, there is a slight chance. Once you know the first person's birthday, there are 365 days left to choose from if there is to be no shared birthday. So the probability of there being *no shared birthday* is 366/366 x 365/366, or 0.997.

The probability of just 2 people sharing a birthday is 1 – 0.997, or only 0.003.

► With three people, the chances are a bit greater: 366/366 x 365/366 x 364/366, or 0.992 of *no shared birthday*, or 0.008 of there being a *shared birthday*.

► For 23 people, you would continue the calculation: 366/366 x 365/366 x 364/366 x 363/366 . . . 345/366 x 344/366.

You will find that the probability of no sharing is 0.494. So the probability of at least one sharing is 1 – 0.494, or 0.506.

Now suppose you were choosing letters of the alphabet randomly instead of birthdays.

Use the model to find the number of letters you need to choose to have a better than 0.50 probability of picking a repeat letter.

Working Daze

Dear Family,
   Our class has studied statistics and graphs. Below are examples of the math skills we have been studying.

Study the frequency chart below and answer the following questions.

Hours per Week at Summer Job

John	24
Pearl	35
Dick	28
Jessie	30
Lamont	35

1. What is the mean of the number of hours worked? _____

2. What is the median of the number of hours worked? _____

3. What is the mode of the number of hours worked? _____

Study the table below and predict the number out of 500 students who would prefer each kind of work.

Summer Jobs
Sample Total: 50 Students

Job	Number of Students
Hospital work	10
Delivering	12
Gardening	5
Office work	7
Baby-sitting	16

4. Hospital work _____

5. Office work _____

6. Gardening _____

7. Baby-sitting _____

8. Delivering _____

Study the circle graph below and answer the following questions.

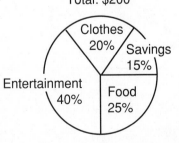

Summer Budget
Total: $200

9. How much is budgeted for food? _____

10. How much is budgeted for savings? _____

11. What is the measure of the central angle for the sector that shows clothes? _____

12. What is the measure of the central angle for the sector that shows entertainment? _____

Name _____

Travel Simulations

World traveler I. M. Weary has just read an unbelievable ad by Fly-by-Night Airlines in his local newspaper. For just $99 round-trip, Fly-by-Night will fly you to any other continent, including Antarctica. The only catch is, because seats are selling so fast, you must be willing to visit the continent that their computer assigns to you. Of course, Weary wants to visit all 6 other continents. He just does not want to have to buy 100 tickets to do it.

How many tickets do you think I. M. will need to buy in order to visit all 6 continents if he is really lucky?

_____

If he is not so lucky?

_____

You can simulate Weary's situation with either a number cube or a spinner marked 1-6. Since each continent has an equal chance of turning up in the computer, assign each continent a number as follows:

Africa 1	Antarctica 2	Asia 3
Australia 4	Europe 5	South America 6

Conduct three trials. In each trial, count the number of tosses or spins used until you have a ticket to each continent. Keep a tally below.

Trial 1		Trial 2		Trial 3	
Africa	_____	Africa	_____	Africa	_____
Antarctica	_____	Antarctica	_____	Antarctica	_____
Asia	_____	Asia	_____	Asia	_____
Australia	_____	Australia	_____	Australia	_____
Europe	_____	Europe	_____	Europe	_____
South America	_____	South America	_____	South America	_____

Baseball Predictions

If your favorite (baseball player) has an average of .250, it means that,

on average, he gets a hit once out of every 4 at-bats. This is because the

fraction $\frac{250}{1000}$ is $\frac{1}{4}$ in lowest terms. So the probability of his getting a hit in

his next at-bat is $\frac{1}{4}$. You can test the reasonableness of this by combining the

two random digit tables on page 350 of your text.

If you look at 3 numbers at a time, there are 1,000 possibilities. The 3-digit
numbers you get can range from 000 to 999. For a .250 hitter, let the numbers
000 through 249 stand for a hit and 250 through 999 stand for an out. By
combining the tables on page 350, you can run 66 simulations of at-bats.

The first 3 numbers are 255. Does this represent a hit or an out? _____

Reading across the first table, how many outs will our batter make

before he gets his first hit? _____

Which digits represent his first hit? _____

How many hits will he get in these 66 simulated at-bats? _____

Is 15 hits in 66 at-bats reasonably close to what you might expect from a .250 hitter?

_____

Suppose as the season nears an end, the player has raised his
average to .333. What is the probability of his getting a hit now? _____

If you ran the same simulation for the player now, what digits

beginning with 000 would stand for a hit? _____ An out? _____

Approximately how many hits would you expect him to have in

his next 66 at-bats? _____

Run the simulation. Are the results about what you expected?

Compatible Exercises

If you run, walk, cycle, or swim, the chart has some information you might find useful. It tells you the pace at which you must exercise to get the same aerobic value from different activities. You can see that if you were to run a mile in 8 minutes or walk a mile in a little more than 10 minutes, or cycle at a little more than 16 miles per hour, or swim a half mile in about 17.5 minutes you would get the same aerobic value.

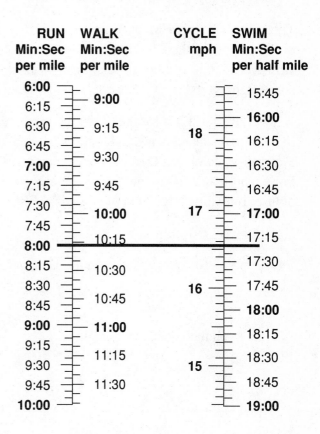

Use the chart to answer these questions.

1. What pace for a half-mile swim is equivalent to running a mile in 10 minutes?

_____

2. At what pace must you run a mile in order to get the same aerobic value you get from walking 1 mi in 9 min?

_____

3. If you swam a full mile in 34 min, how far would you have to walk at a 10-min-mi pace to achieve the same aerobic value?

_____

4. What activity will give you the same aerobic value in 17 min as swimming a half mile in 16 min 35 s?

_____

5. Increasing your cycling speed from 16 to 18 mph is equivalent to lowering your 1-mile running pace from 8 min 15 s to what pace?

_____

Relationships in Space

The angle and line relationships you have studied all occurred within plane or 2-dimensional figures. However, the same kinds of relationships exist within space figures.

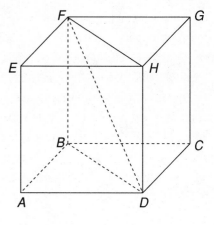

Answer the questions for the cube pictured here. Keep in mind that since this is a 2-dimensional view of a 3-dimensional object, there will be some distortions. For example, ∠*FBD* in the picture appears to be obtuse. In reality, what kind of angle is ∠*FBD*?

_____

1. Can you find an angle that really is an obtuse angle? _____

2. Can you name one acute angle? _____

3. Can you name an angle that is complementary to the angle you named in Question 2?

_____

4. Line segments *HF* and *BD* are parallel. How many transversals cut $\overline{HF}$ and $\overline{BD}$?

_____

5. What can you say about the measures of ∠ *HFD* and ∠ *BDF*? _____

6. Can you name a pair of supplementary angles? _____

_____

7. What shape is figure *HFBD*? _____

Name _____

Another View of Turn Angles

Place your pencil on your desk in front of you. Holding one end in place, rotate the pencil like the hand of a clock until it is in the same position as when you began.

Through how many degrees has your pencil turned?

_____

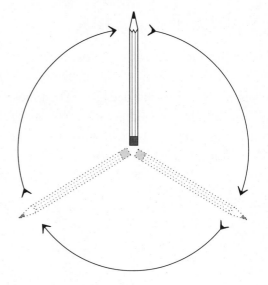

You can use this technique to see that the turn angles of **any** polygon will always add up to 360°.

Follow these steps for the quadrilateral shown here.

Place your pencil along side *AB* with the end on point *A*.
Slide your pencil along *AB* toward *B* until the end is on *B*.
Rotate your pencil through the turn angle at *B* until the pencil lies on side *BC*.
Slide the pencil to *C*, rotate through the turn angle at *C* so the pencil lies on *CD*.
Slide the pencil to *D*, rotate through the turn angle at *D*, and slide the pencil to *A*.
Rotate through the turn angle at *A*.
Do you see that:

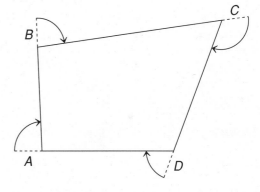

► You have rotated your pencil through all 4 turn angles?

► Your pencil is pointing in the same direction it was when you began your trip around the quadrilateral? If you ignore the slides and think only about the rotations, you will see that this is exactly what you did when you turned your pencil through one complete circle.

Try this technique with any of the pentominoes, remembering to add 90° for a clockwise turn and to subtract 90° for a counterclockwise turn.

What do you think will be the sum of the turn angles

for any pentominoe? _____

Name _____

Regular Polygons

From what you have already learned, complete the table below for a triangle, quadrilateral, pentagon, hexagon, octagon, and decagon. Then look for the pattern in each row and complete the row for an n-gon. (An n-gon is a polygon with any number of sides.) When you have finished, write a generalization in sentence form for each of the 5 entries you have made for an n-gon.

Angles of a Polygon

Polygon	Number of sides	Sum of measures of vertex angles	Each vertex angle of a regular polygon	Sum of turn angles	Each turn angle of a regular polygon
Triangle	3	$180°$	$60°$	$360°$	$120°$
Quadrilateral	4	$360°$	$90°$	$360°$	$90°$
Pentagon	5	$540°$	$108°$	$360°$	$72°$
Hexagon	6	$720°$	$120°$	$360°$	$60°$
Octagon	8	$1,080°$	$135°$	$360°$	$45°$
Decagon	10	$1,440°$	$144°$	$360°$	$36°$
$n-$gon	n	$180°(n-2)$	$\dfrac{180°(n-2)}{n}$	$360°$	$\dfrac{360°}{n}$

Generalizations

1. _____

2. _____

3. _____

4. _____

5. _____

Tessellation Art

An interesting fact about tessellations is that any polygon that will tessellate the plane (cover it with no overlapping) can be changed into another shape that will also tessellate. The one requirement is that the area of the new shape must be identical to the area of the original polygon.

To see this, begin with a tessellating polygon. Find the midpoint of any side.

Draw a curve between the midpoint and one of the vertices.

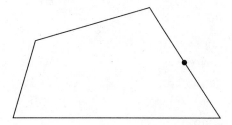

Cut along the curve. Rotate the cut portion around the midpoint and attach it to the other half of the same side.

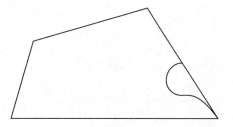

You can leave the new shape as it is; it will tessellate. You can, if you wish, follow the same steps with any or all of the other sides.

Use your imagination to create whatever you wish from your tessellation .

You might be interested in the drawings of M. C. Escher, a Dutch artist who used tessellations in much of his work.

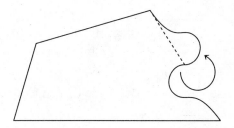

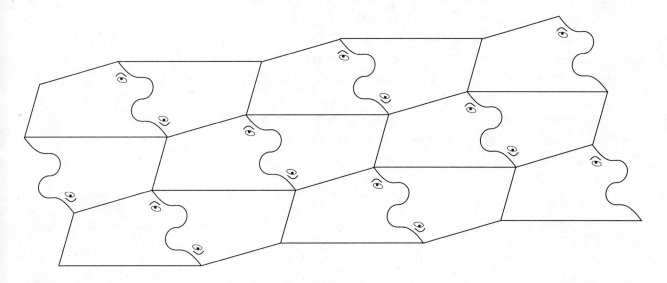

Name _____

Not Another Factory?

Here is another chance to investigate the best
placement for a factory. This story concerns an area
in the shape of an ellipse rather than a triangle.

An ellipse is a special kind of curve. You can draw
an ellipse by following these steps.

Push 2 tacks into a
piece of wood or
heavy cardboard.
Loosely tie a piece
of string around
both tacks. Label
the points *A* and *B*.

Stretch the string
with a pencil and
draw half of the
ellipse.

Stretch the
string again
and draw the
top half of the
ellipse. Remove
the string and
tacks.

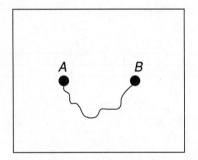
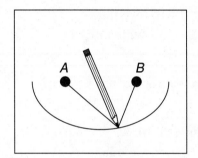
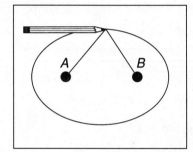

Now use the ellipse you have drawn to solve the
following problem.

The Hungry for Power Electric Company has its generating plant at
point *A*. The company provides electrical power to the city located at
point *B*, about 50 miles away. However, the population of the city is
growing, making it more hungry for power. To meet this demand, the
company is planning to build a substation somewhere on the ellipse.
It will then send power to the substation, which will relay it to the city.
Of course, it wants the total distance that the power must travel—from
the plant to the substation to the city—to be as small as possible. To
meet this condition, where on the ellipse should it build the substation?

_____

_____

_____

Finding π

In each figure, the length $\overline{AB}$ represents the circumference
of (C) of the circle. Measure C and diameter (d) to the
nearest tenth of a centimeter. Then compute $C \div d$ to the
nearest hundredth.

1.

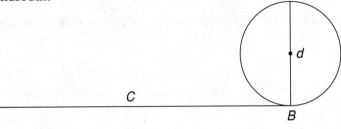

$C =$ _____

$d =$ _____

$C \div d =$ _____

2.

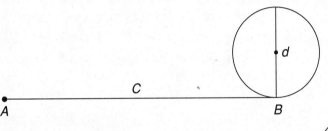

$C =$ _____

$d =$ _____

$C \div d =$ _____

3.

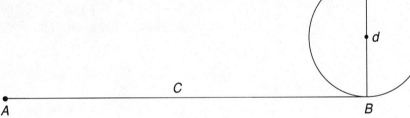

$C =$ _____

$d =$ _____

$C \div d =$ _____

4.

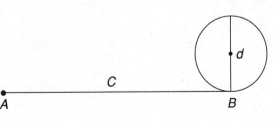

$C =$ _____

$d =$ _____

$C \div d =$ _____

5.

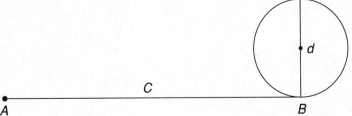

$C =$ _____

$d =$ _____

$C \div d =$ _____

6. What is the average of the five numbers you found for
$C \div d$ in problems 1 through 5? _____

The number should be close to the π, or 3.14159.

Name _____

Drawing to Win

Dear Family,
    We have been studying problem solving in class. This game reinforces the need to follow directions, an important component of successful problem solving.

Number of Players: 4 (two teams of 2)

Materials Needed: pencils or pens, blank paper, 20 index cards or small sheets of paper

How to Play:
Write the name of a different common object on each card (for example, a TV set, lamp, shoe). Mix the cards and turn them facedown.

One member of Team A picks a card, looks at it without allowing his or her teammate to see it, and hands it to a member of Team B, who does the same.

Both players who have seen the card simultaneously give instructions to their teammates to help them draw a picture of the object named on the card. The instructions may consist only of mathematical terms. For example, to get your teammate to draw a television, you might say, "Draw a large rectangle. Draw a rectangle inside the first one. Draw 2 circles inside the first rectangle, but outside the second one," and so on. The member who is drawing must guess what he or she is trying to draw. The first to guess correctly wins the round.

Reverse roles for the next round.

A game may consist of any number of predetermined rounds.

Paper Folding I

Waxed paper is especially good for mathematical folding activities. Folding and creasing waxed paper has two advantages over other kinds of paper:

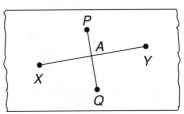

► It is transparent, so you can see exactly where you need to fold it, and

► When creased, it leaves a clearly seen white line.

Try this activity to create a pair of parallel segments.

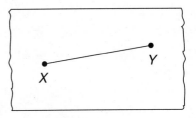

1. Tear off a sheet of waxed paper about one foot long. Fold a crease anywhere on the paper. Call the crease line segment *XY*.

2. Fold *X* over until it is exactly on *Y* and crease the paper. Open it and label the second crease *PQ*. Label the intersection *A*.

3. Fold point *Q* over until it lies right on the intersection of line segments *XY* and *PQ*. Crease the paper. Then open it and label the new segment *RS*. Label the new intersection *B*.

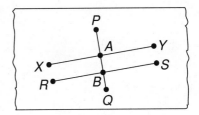

What is the relationship between:

Line segments *XY* and *PQ*? _____

The lengths of segments *AB* and *BQ*? _____

Line segments *XY* and *RS*? _____

The lengths of segments *XA* and *AY*? _____

Perpendicular Bisectors

The perpendicular bisectors of the sides of a triangle will always intersect at a point. However, the point at which they meet depends on the kind of triangle. Look at the triangles below and try to visualize the perpendicular bisectors. Then complete each sentence with **inside**, **outside**, or **on**.

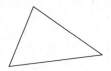 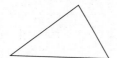   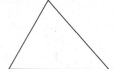

The perpendicular bisectors of the sides of any acute

triangle intersect _____ the triangle.

The perpendicular bisectors of the sides of any right

triangle intersect _____ the triangle.

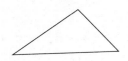 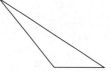 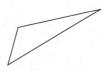 

The perpendicular bisectors of the sides of any

obtuse triangle intersect _____ the triangle.

Now check your estimates. Enlarge several of each type of triangle. Use paper folding to construct the perpendicular bisectors of each side.

Do they always meet at a point? _____

Do they meet where you expected? _____

Name _____

The Need for Education

The double bar graph shows how the level of education needed for jobs has changed. Use information from the graph to answer the questions.

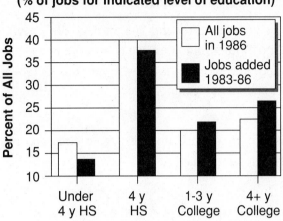

The Growing Demand for Education
(% of jobs for indicated level of education)

1. What is the most commonly required level of education for all jobs? For jobs added since 1983?

_____

_____

2. For which levels of education does the percent of available jobs seem to be decreasing? Increasing?

_____

_____

_____

_____

3. Which level of education underwent the largest percent change in new jobs as compared to all jobs?

_____

_____

4. Approximately what percent of all jobs require 4 or more years of college?

_____

New jobs?

_____

5. What is the approximate percent increase in new jobs requiring 4 or more years of college as compared to all jobs?

_____

6. If the percent increase from Question 5 continues each year, approximately how many years will pass until more than half of all jobs require 4 or more years of college?

_____

7. Write a sentence that summarizes the data in this graph.

_____

_____

_____

Paper Folding III

A curve like the second one on page 382 of your text is called a **parabola**. You see this curve in many places: the path of a batted or thrown ball, the arch of a suspension bridge, the reflection of a flashlight.

Every parabola has a property that you can discover through paper folding.

Crease a line segment *AB* on a sheet of waxed paper. mark a point *C* several inches from the segment.

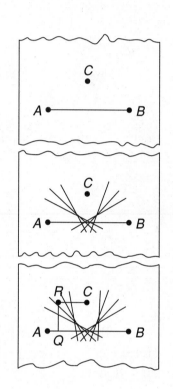

Fold the point onto the line segment and crease. Move the point along the segment and crease again. Do this 15 or 20 times.

Do you see the curve beginning to appear?

Mark any point on the curve. Call it *R*. Measure the length of segment *CR*.

Draw a segment from *R* perpendicular to *AB*. Measure the length of segment *RQ*.

What do you notice about the lengths of *CR* and *RQ*? _____

Mark several other points on the parabola. Measure the distances to the focus point (*C*) and the directrix (*AB*). What do you predict will be true for any parabola?

_____

_____

_____

_____

Measures of Polygons

Find the missing dimensions from the picture below.

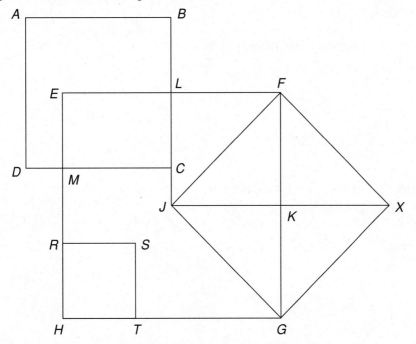

1. Area of square *ABCD* = 16 square cm. Length of side *AD* = _____

2. Length of *FG* = 6 cm. Area of square *EFGH* = _____

3. Length of *JK* = 3 cm. Area of square *KJLF* = _____

4. Area of rectangle *ELCM* = 6 cm². Area of polygon *ABLEMD* = _____

5. Area of square *HRST* = 4 cm². Length of side *RS* = _____

6. Area of polygon *MCJKGTSR* = _____

7. Length of *KX* = 3 cm. Area of triangle *KFX* = _____

8. Measure the length of segment *FX*. Use this length to estimate

the area of square *GJFX*. _____

9. How does your estimate of the area of square *GJFX* in Problem 8 compare to the area of the

square found by multiplying the area of triangle *KFX* by 4? _____

_____

_____

Finding Square Roots Geometrically

You can estimate the square root of the length of any
line segment by following these steps:

xy = 5 cm yz = 1 cm

1. Draw a segment of a given length, say, 5 cm.
   Extend the segment 1 cm farther.

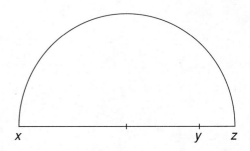

2. Find the midpoint of segment XZ. Use the
   midpoint to draw a semicircle that has XZ
   as a diameter.

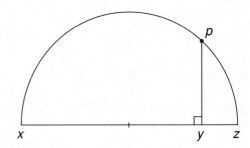

3. Draw a segment perpendicular to XZ at Y that
   intersects the semicircle.

4. Measure the length of YP as accurately as possible.
   This length is a good estimate of the square root of
   length XY.

   _____

   Does your estimate for the square root of the length
   of the original segment seem reasonable? You can
   test your estimate using the square root key on your
   calculator.

Estimate the square roots of segments of the following
lengths using this method:

A 7 cm   **B** 10 cm   **C** 8.5 cm

_____   _____   _____

Heron's Area Formula

Suppose you wanted to measure the area of the plot of land shown here. The pond prevents you from measuring any altitude of the triangle. Therefore, you cannot use the formula $A = \frac{1}{2} b \times h$. What would you do?

Fortunately there is an alternative. The ancient Greek mathematician Heron developed a formula for the area of any triangle when only the lengths of the three sides are known.

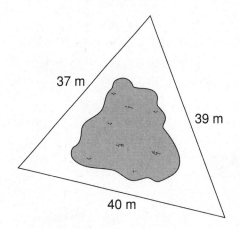

Here is the formula:

Area $= \sqrt{s(s-a)(s-b)(s-c)}$
where $s = \frac{1}{2}$ the perimeter of the triangle and a, b, and c are the lengths of the sides.

For the plot of land:
$A = \sqrt{58(58-37)(58-39)(58-40)}$
$= \sqrt{58 \times 21 \times 19 \times 18}$
$= \sqrt{416,556}$
$= 645.412 \text{ m}^2$

Use Heron's formula and the square root key on your calculator to find the area of each triangle.
Write *rational* or *irrational* to describe each area.

1.

6 m 10 m 8 m

_____

_____

2.

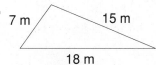

7 m 15 m 18 m

_____

_____

3. 14 m

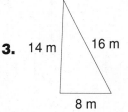

16 m 8 m

_____

_____

4. 28 m, 30 m, 36 m

_____

_____

5. 10 m, 24 m, 26 m

_____

_____

A Reading Assignment

An eighth-grade student noticed that during the school year she had read books of certain lengths. She drew graphs describing the number of pages in each book.

Read each description. Then write the letter of the appropriate graph next to its description.

► A book with more than or fewer than 150 pages _____

► A book with more than 150 pages _____

► A book with fewer than 150 pages _____

► A book with either 150 pages or more than 150 pages _____

► A book with either 150 pages or fewer than 150 pages _____

► A book with 150 pages _____

► A book with fewer than 150 pages but more than 130 pages _____

► A book with more than 150 pages but fewer than 170 pages _____

A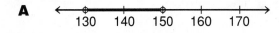

B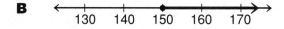

C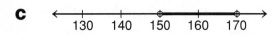

D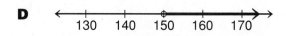

E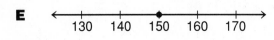

F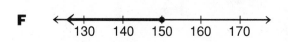

G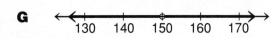

H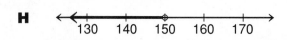

Figure This Out

Work with a friend. Analyze each pair of diagrams.
Then write a definition of each new term.

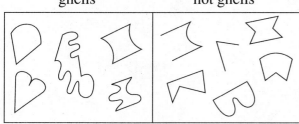

A gnell is _____

_____

_____

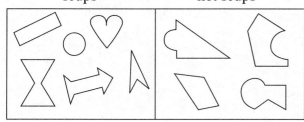

A scup is _____

_____

_____

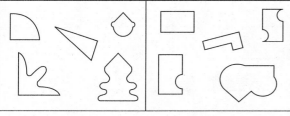

A ziote is _____

_____

_____

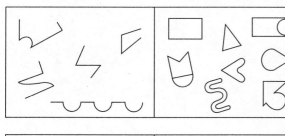

A knute is _____

_____

_____

Now try to stump a friend. Think of a new
term and draw shapes in the boxes. Have your
friend guess the definition.

Name _____

Did You Lose a Hypotenuse?

Find the missing hypotenuse of each triangle. You may
use a calculator. Round to the nearest tenth.

1.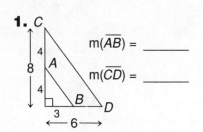

m($\overline{AB}$) = _____

m($\overline{CD}$) = _____

2.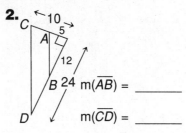

m($\overline{AB}$) = _____

m($\overline{CD}$) = _____

3.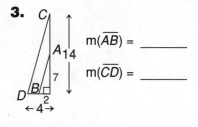

m($\overline{AB}$) = _____

m($\overline{CD}$) = _____

4.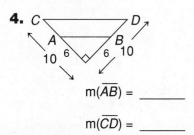

m($\overline{AB}$) = _____

m($\overline{CD}$) = _____

5.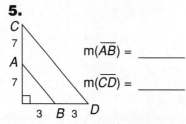

m($\overline{AB}$) = _____

m($\overline{CD}$) = _____

6.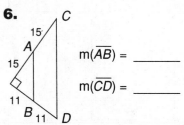

m($\overline{AB}$) = _____

m($\overline{CD}$) = _____

7. Look at each pair of triangles above. Compare the sides of
the larger triangle to those of the smaller. What conclusions
can you draw?

_____

_____

_____

Find the missing hypotenuse of each triangle. You may use a
calculator. Round to the nearest tenth.

8.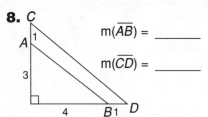

m($\overline{AB}$) = _____

m($\overline{CD}$) = _____

9.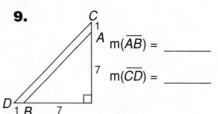

m($\overline{AB}$) = _____

m($\overline{CD}$) = _____

10.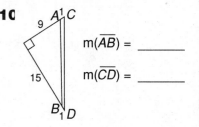

m($\overline{AB}$) = _____

m($\overline{CD}$) = _____

11. Does adding 1 to each leg increase the
hypotenuse by 1?

_____

Answers Plus!

Work with a partner. Use any problem solving strategy.

1. The bicycle repair shop repairs tricycles and bicycles. Yesterday the shop used 58 wheels. How many bicycles and tricycles were repaired?

_____
_____
_____

2. At the farm, there are ducks and cows. Farmer Jones counted 34 legs. How many ducks and cows were there?

_____
_____
_____

3. The Shape Company manufactures geometric figures. All are made from wooden strips the same length. Last week squares and equivalent triangles were manufactured. Exactly 671 wooden strips were used. How many triangles and squares were manufactured?

_____
_____
_____

4. The carpenter builds 3 different plant stands—with 3, 4, or 5 shelves. All shelves are identical circles. Last Friday she used 95 shelves. How many of each plant stand did she make?

_____
_____
_____

5. Look back at the problems above.

A How are they different ? _____

_____

B How are they the same ? _____

_____

C What problem solving strategies helped you solve the problems ?

_____
_____

Geoboard Challenges

Use a geoboard and rubber band to construct 45°- 45°
right triangles with the given dimensions. Fill in any
missing dimensions. Then draw them on the dot paper.

1. Legs: 1 unit

Hypotenuse: _____ units

2. Legs: $\sqrt{2}$ units

Hypotenuse: _____ units

3. Legs: 2 units

Hypotenuse: _____ units

4. Legs: $2\sqrt{2}$ units

Hypotenuse: _____ units

5. Legs: _____ units

Hypotenuse: $4\sqrt{2}$ units

6. Legs: $\sqrt{5}$ units

Hypotenuse: _____ units

A Geometric Model of Pythagoras

For any right triangle, the square of the hypotenuse is equal to the sum of the squares of the legs. The geometric model for that equality states that the **area** of the square **on** the hypotenuse is equal to the sum of the **areas** of the squares **on** the legs.

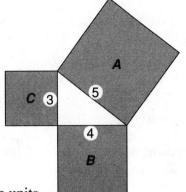

You can see this in the picture.

Area A = Area B + Area C or

_____ square units = _____ square units + _____ square units

It may surprise you to find that the same geometric model will work with figures other than squares. The only requirement is that the figures on the sides of the triangle must be similar to one another. Since all semicircles are similar, you can test whether the model will work with that figure.

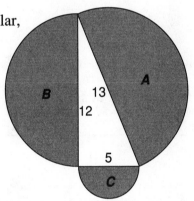

$13^2 = 12^2 + 5^2$, therefore,

Area A = _____

Area B = _____

Area C = _____

Remember that these are **semi**circles.

Does the geometric model work using semicircles? _____

Can you name another figure that would demonstrate

the Pythagorean theorem as did semicircles? _____

_____

_____

_____

Horsing Around

Set up the equations necessary to solve the following
problems. Then use your calculator to do the computation.

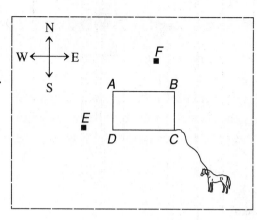

A horse is in a corral tied to the corner of a barn.
The rope holding the horse is 25 feet long.
The barn is 20 feet long by 12 feet wide.

1. A bale of hay is at point *E*, 6 feet west and
1 foot north of point *D*.

Can the horse reach the bale in order to graze on it? _____

How do you know? _____

_____

2. How many more feet of rope would be needed for the horse to be able

to reach the bale at point *E*? _____

_____

3. Another bale of hay is located at point *F*, which is exactly 5 feet west
and 12 feet north of point *B*. Can the horse reach this bale?

Explain. _____

4. How much area inside the corral does the horse have to
graze on while he is tied to the rope?

_____

_____

Coordinate Translations

Draw and label axes on centimeter graph paper.
Then copy the polygon onto the grid.

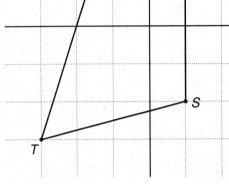

Write the coordinates of each vertex of the polygon:

Q: (_____, _____)   R: (_____, _____)

S: (_____, _____)   T: (_____, _____)

Now draw slide images of the polygon that meet the
following conditions:

1. All coordinates contain only positive integers.

2. All coordinates contain only negative integers.

3. The first integer of each coordinate is negative,
   the second positive.

4. The first integer of each coordinate is positive,
   the second negative.

Complete the description of each slide image you have drawn:

1. (x, y) $>(x +$ _____$, y +$ _____$)$

2. (x, y) $>(x -$ _____$, y -$ _____$)$

3. (x, y) $>(x -$ _____$, y +$ _____$)$

4. (x, y) $>(x +$ _____$, y -$ _____$)$

Name _____

Coordinate Reflections

The coordinates of polygon *ABCD* after a transformation are given below:

A' : (2, 1) B' : (1, $^-$3)

C' :(5, $^-$3) D' : (7, 1)

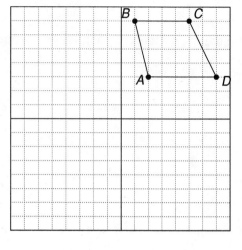

1. Draw the image polygon $A'B'C'D'$.

2. What type of transformation creates image polygon $A'B'C'D'$?

_____

3. Draw the reflection line on the coordinate grid.

_____

4. Give the points for the polygon $A''B''C''D''$ if you reflect $A'B'C'D'$ over the y–axis.

_____

5. Make your own reflection and describe it.

_____

Rotation Patterns

On page 424 of your text you found a rule for finding the coordinates of a point (x,y) following a $\frac{1}{2}$ **clockwise** turn.

What are the coordinates of point (x,y) following this turn? _____

Use the same principle to find the coordinates following these two rotations:

1. A $\frac{1}{4}$ turn **counterclockwise** around point $(0,0)$

Original Coordinates	Coordinates After Turn
$A\ (2,1)$	_____
$B\ (3,^-1)$	_____
$C\ (5,2)$	_____
$D\ (2,4)$	_____

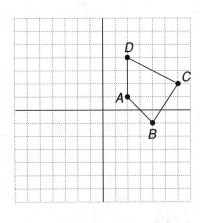

Describe the coordinates of point (x,y) following a $\frac{1}{2}$ turn counterclockwise around $(0,0)$.

_____

2. A $\frac{1}{2}$ turn around point $(0,0)$

Original Coordinates	Coordinates After Turn
$A\ (3,^-2)$	_____
$B\ (1,0)$	_____
$C\ (^-1,^-3)$	_____
$D\ (2,^-4)$	_____

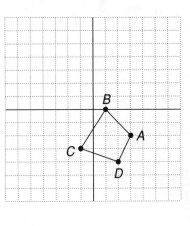

Describe the coordinates of point (x,y) after a $\frac{1}{2}$ turn around point $(0,0)$. _____

Symmetric Designs

A symmetric design can be made by placing numbers on
a grid in a pattern. Look for the pattern in the coordinates
in the table below. Plot the points on the grid. Connect
the points by drawing lines. Draw a line between the last
point and first point to complete the design.

| **1.** (12, 0) | **2.** (⁻2, 6) | **3.** (0, ⁻12) | **4.** (⁻12, 0) | **5.** (2, ⁻6) | **6.** (0, 12) |
| **7.** (⁻12, 0) | **8.** (2, 6) | **9.** (0, ⁻12) | **10.** (12, 0) | **11.** (⁻2, ⁻6) | **12.** (0, 12) |

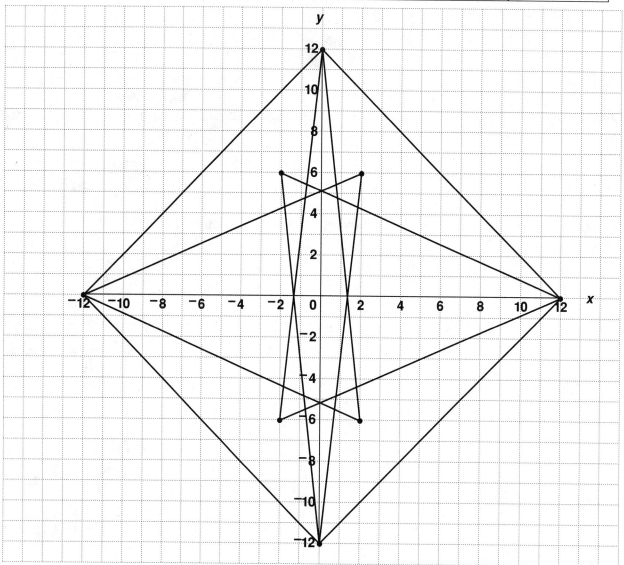

On a sheet of graph paper, make your own table of coordinates.
Try to make a symmetric design. Plot your coordinates on the grid.

Proving Congruence

Each pair of triangles is congruent. Write a sentence that explains how you could prove their congruence through one or more transformations.

1.

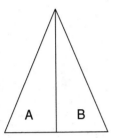

_____

_____

2.

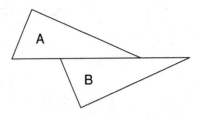

_____

_____

_____

3.

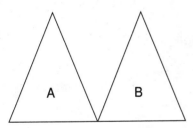

_____

4.

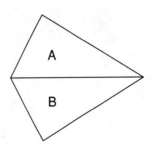

_____

_____

5.

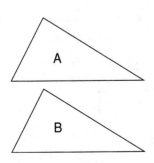

_____

6.

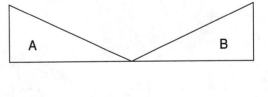

_____

_____

_____

Symmetrical Figures

You can use the Logo computer language to complete symmetrical figures. The solid-line figure on the screen was drawn using the following procedure:

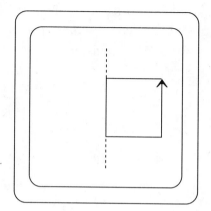

Left 90	Forward 50
Left 90	Forward 50
Left 90	Forward 50
Left 90	Forward 50

You can draw the reflection image across the dotted line using this procedure:

LT 90 FD 100 LT 90 FD 50 LT 90 FD 50

Use Logo to draw each figure on the screen. Then write a procedure to draw the reflection image across the dotted line. Begin with the turtle in the position shown.

1.
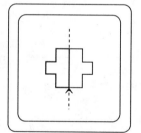
LT 90 FD 20
RT 90 FD 20

2.
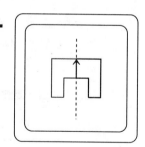
RT 90 FD 80
RT 90 FD 80

3.
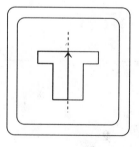

4.
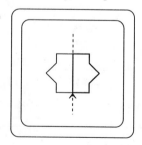

Use with text pages 430–431.

Coordinate Graphs

For each pair of expressions:

► Translate each English statement into an algebraic expression.

► Draw a graph of each equation on a coordinate grid.

► Write the coordinates of the point of intersection, if there is one.

1. A. The sum of the x and y coordinates is 7. _____

B. The y coordinate is one less than the x coordinate. _____

_____

2. A. The difference between the x and y coordinates is 4. _____

B. The value of the x coordinate is 6. _____

_____

3. A. The y coordinate is twice the x coordinate. _____

B. The y coordinate is 2 more than the x coordinate. _____

_____

4. A. The x and y coordinates are equal. _____

B. The y coordinate is half the x coordinate. _____

_____

5. A. The y coordinate is 1 less than twice the x. _____

B. The value of the y coordinate is 3. _____

_____

As the Crow Does Not Fly

Arthur drew a grid like the one at the right. He asked his brother to help him figure the shortest path along the grid lines from A to B. Then he wanted to know how many other routes there were that were just as short.

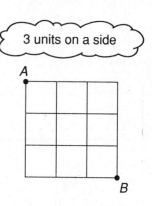

3 units on a side

His brother decided to start with a drawing of a simpler problem.

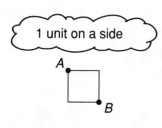

1 unit on a side

Starting at A the shortest route is to move along the grid to the right or down.

The shortest route is **2** unit lengths.

There are **2** routes that are equally short.

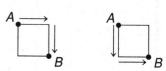

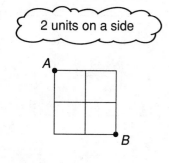

2 units on a side

Again move each time to the right or down.

The shortest route is **4** unit lengths.

There are **6** routes that are equally short.

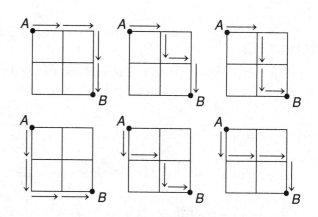

1. Use a separate sheet of paper to draw as many 3-unit-length squares as needed to determine the number of units in the shortest route and the number of equally short routes.

_____

_____

Name _____

A Regular Polygon Construction

Follow the step-by-step directions
using the angle and line segment shown
here. When you see the pattern
developing, complete the regular
polygon.

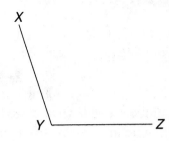

1. On a sheet of unlined paper, construct a horizontal
   segment congruent to $\overline{AB}$. Label the segment $\overline{XY}$.

2. At point A construct an angle congruent to $< XYZ$ using
   $\overline{AB}$ as one of the rays.

3. Mark off a length equal to $\overline{AB}$ on the other ray and call
   the new endpoint C. $\overline{AB} = \overline{AC}$.

4. At point C construct an angle congruent to $< XYZ$ using
   $\overline{AC}$ as one of the rays.

5. Mark off a length equal to $\overline{AC}$ and call the new endpoint
   D. $\overline{AC} = \overline{AD}$

6. At point D construct an angle congruent to $< XYZ$ using
   $\overline{CD}$ as one of the rays.

7. Mark off a length equal to $\overline{CD}$ and call the new endpoint
   E. $\overline{CD} = \overline{DE}$.

8. Draw $\overline{DE}$. If you have done the constructions carefully,
   $\overline{DE}$ should be congruent to $\overline{AB}$.

What regular polygon do these directions lead you to?

_____

Demonstrating Congruence

Congruent figures can be traced, cut out, and made to coincide to test their congruence.

For the pairs of congruent triangles below, trace and cut out the second. Then place the cutout on top of the first triangle in as many different ways as possible to show congruence. Keep a list of the triangles that coincide with the first one. You will have to flip the cutouts to take account of all possibilities.

1. Isosceles

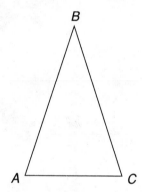
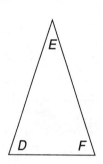

Triangle *ABC* can be matched with

_____

_____

2. Equilateral

Triangle *RST* can be matched with

_____

_____

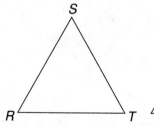
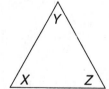

Geo-Congruent Triangles

Each geoboard contains a pair of congruent triangles.
For each pair, describe how you would demonstrate their
congruence. If the congruence cannot be shown, state that.

1.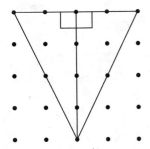

_____

2.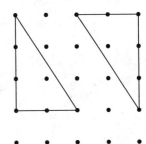

_____

3.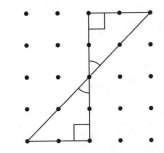

_____

4.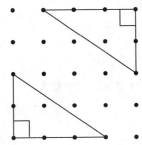

_____

5.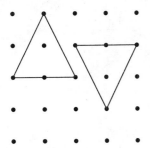

_____

6.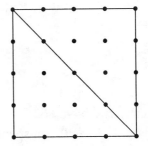

_____

Lunchtime Decisions

Look at the data in the menu to the right.
Then read each of the problems based on the
data. Write a sentence telling the plan you
would use to solve the problem.

Burger Haven			
Burger	$0.95	Fries	$0.60
Double burger	$1.75	Large fries	$0.79
Cheeseburger	$1.30	Onion rings	$1.35
Double		Juice	$0.45
Cheeseburger	$1.95	Large juice	$0.70

1. If you ordered a burger and a large juice,
how much would your bill be?

_____

_____

_____

2. If you buy a double cheeseburger and
onion rings, how much change will you
get from $5.00?

_____

_____

_____

3. Suppose you order 2 burgers, 2 fries, and
a juice. What will the cost be?

_____

_____

_____

_____

_____

4. Your bill was exactly $2.70. What did
you have for lunch?

_____

_____

_____

_____

_____

5. You and a friend have $6.00 to spend on lunch for
both of you. How will you spend the money?

_____

_____

Number Series

In each number series below, the following applies:

S = the sum of all the numbers
f = the first number
l = the last number
n = the number of terms in the series

Examine each series and the formula given for its sum. Then find the sum two ways: using induction and using the formula.

1. $1 + 2 + 3 + 4 + \ldots + 24 + 25$ $S = \dfrac{n(n+1)}{2}$ _____

2. $5 + 7 + 9 + 11 + \ldots + 35 + 37$ $S = \dfrac{n}{2}(f + l)$ _____

3. $2 + 4 + 6 + 8 + \ldots + 98 + 100$ $S = n(n + 1)$ _____

4. $20 + 21 + 22 + 23 + \ldots + 79 + 80$ $S = \dfrac{n(n+1)}{2}$ _____

5. $1^2 + 2^2 + 3^2 + 4^2 + \ldots + 9^2 + 10^2$ $S = \dfrac{n(n+1)(2n+1)}{6}$ _____

6. $5 + 10 + 15 + 20 + \ldots + 95 + 100$ $S = \dfrac{n}{2}(f + l)$ _____

A Number of Shapes

Numbers that can be displayed as a square figure are
referred to as square numbers.

What is the fifth square number? _____ The tenth? _____
Use induction to determine the fifteenth number in each series.
For each series, describe how you arrived at your answer.

Triangular Numbers 1

1.

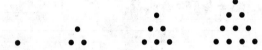

_____

Triangular Numbers 2

2.

_____

Pentagonal Numbers

3.

_____

Rectangular Numbers

4.

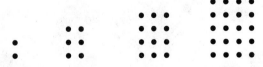

_____

Perfect and Friendly Numbers

Over the centuries, fascinating relationships between numbers have been discovered. Among these are relationships involving two kinds of numbers: perfect numbers and friendly numbers.

From the information below, try to figure out what makes perfect numbers "perfect" and when two numbers are "friendly."

1. The first two perfect numbers are 6 and 28.
The factors of each number (including itself) are:
6: 1, 2, and 3   28: 1, 2, 4, 7, 14

What is the sum of these factors of 6? _____ Of 28? _____
Which of these is the next perfect number? Ring it.   495   496   497

How did you decide? _____

_____

2. The first pair of friendly numbers is 220 and 284.
Write the factors of each (excluding itself).

220: _____

284: _____

What do you find when you add these factors of each number? _____

_____

Test your theory on this pair of friendly numbers: 1,184 and 1,210.

Puzzles

Using only the keys 4, +, −, ×, ÷, and =, obtain the
number 7.

How many operations did it take you? _____

Write your equation here: _____

Using only four 4s and the keys +, −, ×, ÷, and =,
write 5 different equations.

How many different answers can you get?

Equation	Answer
1. _____	_____
2. _____	_____
3. _____	_____
4. _____	_____
5. _____	_____

Can there be different equations to get the same answer? _____

Enter a 3-digit number into your calculator.

Repeat those 3 digits to give you a 6-digit number.

Divide that by 13.

Divide that answer by 11.

Now divide by 7.

Your final answer should be your original 3-digit number.

Can you find any exceptions? _____

Name _____

There Are a Number of Factors

You can find the number of factors of any number by
using prime factorization.

How many factors does 320 have? _____

Find the prime factors using a tree.

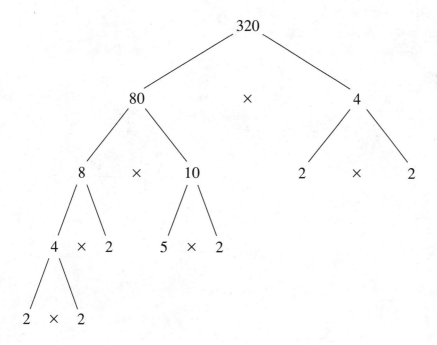

$$320 = 2 \times 2 \times 2 \times 2 \times 2 \times 2 \times 5$$

$$320 = 2^{6} \times 5^{1}$$

The number of factors of 320 is $(6 + 1) \times (1 + 1) = 7 \times 2 = 14$.

(1, 2, 4, 5, 8, 10, 16, 20, 32, 40, 64, 80, 160, 320)

Use prime factorization to find the number of factors
of each number.

1. 150 _____

2. 260 _____

3. 83 _____

4. 1,000 _____

5. 540 _____

6. 76 _____

7. 600 _____

8. 175 _____

9. 210 _____

10. 300 _____

11. 171 _____

12. 143 _____

Arithmetic and Geometric Sequences

An **arithmetic** sequence is one in which the difference
between each term and the preceding one is a constant.
A **geometric** sequence is one in which the quotient of
each term and the preceding one is a constant.
For each sequence below, write **arithmetic,**
geometric, or **neither.** Then, if possible, write the next
3 terms of the sequence. Examine each sequence
carefully, since it may not be possible to extend each
one. If impossible, write **impossible.**

1. 1   1   2   3   5   8   13   21 _____ _____ _____ _____

2. 1   3   6   10   15   21 _____ _____ _____ _____

3. 2   6   18   54   162 _____ _____ _____ _____

4. 600   120   30   10   5   5 _____ _____ _____ _____

5. 6.5   7.2   7.9   8.6   9.3 _____ _____ _____ _____

6. 2   ⁻4   8   ⁻16   32 _____ _____ _____ _____

7. 10   ⁻50   200   ⁻600   1,200   ⁻1,200 _____ _____ _____ _____

8. 2 $\frac{1}{2}$ 3 $\frac{3}{4}$ 5   6 $\frac{1}{4}$ 7 _____ _____ _____ _____

Name _____

Not-So-Magic-Tricks

Each set of instructions is the generalized form of a
number trick like the ones on page 464 of your text.
Suppose you wanted to perform the tricks for a friend.
For each trick, write the directions you would give
your friend at each step.

1. n _____

$n + 5$ _____

$3n + 15$ _____

$3n + 9$ _____

$n + 3$ _____

3 _____

_____

_____

2. n _____

$n - 2$ _____

$4n - 8$ _____

$2n - 4$ _____

$2n$ _____

2 _____

_____

_____

3. n _____

$n + (n - 1)$ _____

_____

$(2n - 1) + 7$ _____

$n + 3$ _____

3 _____

_____

_____

4. n _____

$n - 2$ _____

$3n - 6$ _____

$3n$ _____

n _____

0 _____

_____

_____

5. Create and test a series of instructions like the ones
above. When you are satisfied that they will produce
the same answer regardless of the number you begin

with, try them on a friend. _____

Name _____

A New Area Formula

You have found the area of a rectangle, a square, a parallelogram, a trapezoid, and a triangle by using a variety of formulas. It is also possible to find the areas of each of these figures using one formula, the midline formula. The midline of a polygon is a line parallel to the bases midway between them. Here is the derivation:

A rectangle $= b \times h$; $b =$ midline, so $\boldsymbol{A = mh}$

A square $= s^2$ or $s \times h$; $s =$ midline, so $\boldsymbol{A = mh}$

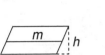

A parallelogram $= b \times h$; $b =$ midline, so $\boldsymbol{A = mh}$

A trapezoid $= \frac{1}{2}(b_1 + b_2)h$; $\frac{1}{2}(b_1 + b_2) = m$; so $\boldsymbol{A = mh}$

A triangle $= \frac{1}{2}b \times h$; $\dfrac{b_1 + b_2}{2} = m$, so $\boldsymbol{A = mh}$

Use the midline formula to find the areas.

1.   Midline = _____

Area = _____

_____

2. 21   Midline = _____

11   Area = _____

_____

3. 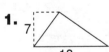 13   Midline = _____

Area = _____

_____

4. 12   Midline = _____

9   Area = _____

20

_____

Name _____

Birth Rates

The chart shows the percent of babies born by the end of each month in an average year. Answer as many questions as you can from the data in the chart. Then construct a line graph to answer the remaining questions.

Percent of babies born in the U.S. by the end of:	
January	8.2 percent
February	15.9 percent
March	24.2 percent
April	32.2 percent
May	40.4 percent
June	48.5 percent
July	57.2 percent
August	66.1 percent
September	74.9 percent
October	83.5 percent
November	91.5 percent
December	100.0 percent

1. Without calculating, predict which month is likely to have the least number of babies born.

_____

2. Justify your answer to Question 1.

_____

3. Now check your prediction. Were you correct?

_____

4. Suppose 5,000,000 babies are born in a given year. During which month would you expect the following babies to be born?

A the 500,000th _____

B the 2,500,000th _____

C the 1,500,000th _____

D the 4,000,000th _____

5. Which month accounts for the largest percent of births?

_____

6. Does the percent of births remain constant between any two consecutive months?

_____

7. Between which pairs of months does the percent of babies born increase? Decrease?

_____

_____

_____

_____

_____

_____

_____

A Graphic Amusement Park

Six enjoyable (for some people) amusement park
activities are shown below. Each graph represents the
movement pattern that is typical for the activity.

Spend some time at the park and match each graph
with one of these activities:

► old-fashioned whip► Ferris wheel ► merry-go-round
► snack bar ► water flume ► walk-through haunted house

1.

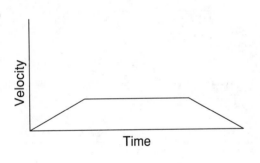

_____

2.

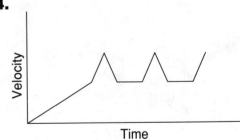

_____

3.

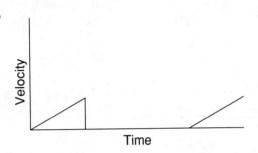

_____

4.

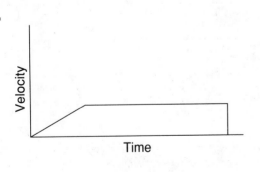

_____

5.

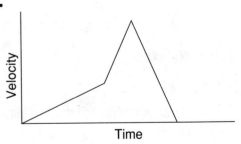

_____

6.

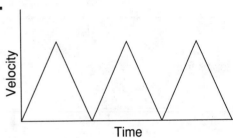

_____

Name _____

Estimation Problems

Rob and Laura were working on their homework. They
remembered to estimate before solving each problem.
However, their estimates caused more problems than
they solved. Read each problem and their reasoning.
Then explain the mistake they made.

1. An airline whose planes each seat 175
people has 1,200 tickets sold for a certain
day. How many planes must be readied
for the day's flights if each plane will be

filled to capacity? _____

Their reasoning: Round 175 up to 200.
Since 1,200 is a multiple of 200, divide
mentally to find that 6 planes will be
needed.

_____

_____

_____

_____

2. The catering department of the airline
prepares lunches. If meals are always
prepared in batches of 110, how many
batches are needed for the 1,200

passengers? _____

Their reasoning: Round 110 down to 100.
Since 100 is a factor of 1,200, divide
mentally to find that 12 batches of meals
will have to be prepared.

_____

_____

_____

_____